East Florida in the Revolutionary Era

East Florida in the Revolutionary Era

1763–1785

George Kotlik

NewSouth Books
an imprint of
The University of Georgia Press
Athens

NSB

Published by NewSouth Books
an imprint of the University of Georgia Press
Athens, Georgia 30602
www.ugapress.org/imprints/newsouth-books/

Printed and bound by Books International

The paper in this book meets the guidelines for permanence and durability of the Committee on Production Guidelines for Book Longevity of the Council on Library Resources.

Most NewSouth/University of Georgia Press titles are available from popular e-book vendors.

Printed in the United States of America
22 23 24 25 26 P 5 4 3 2 1

Library of Congress Control Number: 2022944404
ISBN: 9781588384720 (hardback)
ISBN: 9781588385024 (paperback)
ISBN: 9781588384867 (ebook)

To my parents.

I could not have written this book without you.

Contents

East Florida in the Revolutionary Era

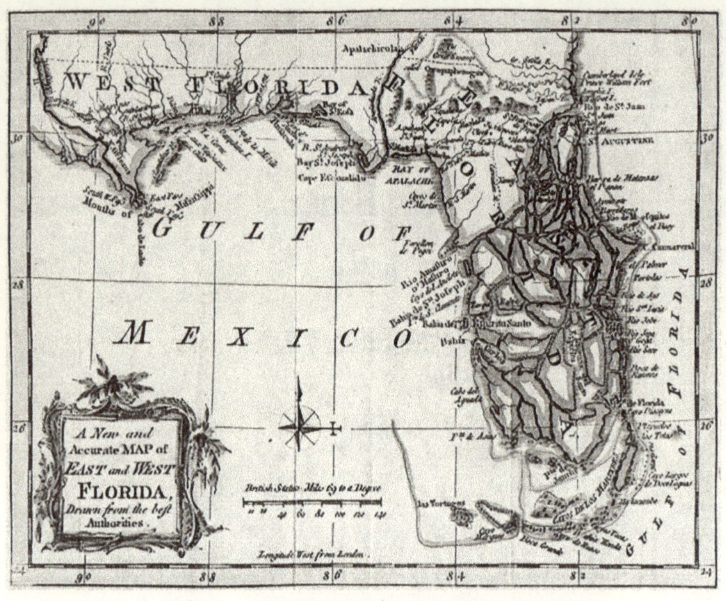

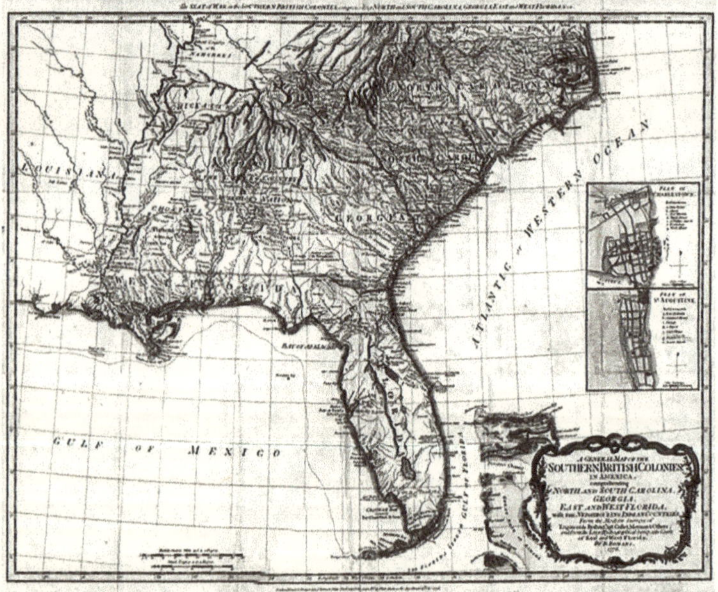

Top, 1763 map of East and West Florida; bottom, 1776 map of the Southern British Colonies (both courtesy of the State Archives of Florida).

Introduction

"It is an Object of considerable importance, & if it could be effected, would produce the most valuable & salutary consequences," General George Washington wrote in 1777.[1] He was referring to St. Augustine, East Florida's capital during the British colonial period. During the American Revolutionary War, Washington, like many patriot leaders, particularly those in Georgia, sought to bring East Florida into the rebellion. Today, the story of British East Florida exists on the fringes of Revolutionary War era scholarship. Most research on the American Revolution deals primarily with the original thirteen colonies. Often forgotten is that by 1775, the British Empire boasted thirty-three colonies in the Americas.[2] Historians and authors usually mention the original thirteen British colonies in reference to the American Revolution. Yet East Florida can be thought of as the "fourteenth colony," and was significant during that time period and conflict. When Britain acquired Florida from Spain after the Seven Years' War (also known as the French and Indian War, 1754–1763), British leadership divided that territory into two separate provinces: East and West. St. Augustine became the capital of East Florida and Pensacola the capital of West Florida. A lone dirt road hacked through the thick Florida wilderness connected the two provinces.[3] Known by the Spanish as El Camino Real, it was the only overland route over Florida. Regarding both East and West Florida, historians usually have written only about one or the other.

In contemporary scholarship, the American Revolution has received much attention. Monographs on the northern theater of the war dominate historical literature. Historians are so apt to write about the exploits of the original thirteen colonies that they have almost written East Florida entirely out of the American Revolutionary War narrative. At best, East Florida is briefly mentioned. At worst, it is not mentioned at all, at least not to anyone who lives outside of Florida. It is unfortunate that the history of Florida's role in the United States' founding has been reduced to near anonymity. Such existence along the far-flung fringes of literature, away from any recognition, leads one to assume that nothing important happened in Florida during the Revolution. No statement is further from the truth. East Florida was a hotbed of Revolutionary War activity. Indeed, it was the site of a few significant battles, constituting part of the southern theater of the war; it was a loyalist haven for refugees fleeing rebel violence; it served as a barrier colony, protecting British sugar plantations in the West Indies from the anti-British movement; and most importantly, it was a thorn in the side of the rebellious southern states during the war, threatening Georgia's invasion on numerous occasions.

To date, few published books have covered British East Florida in the American Revolutionary Era.[4] During the first half of the twentieth century, East Florida received little scholarly attention. Nothing significant on eighteenth-century East Florida was published until in the 1970s, when the Florida Bicentennial

Commission, celebrating the bicentennial of the adoption of the Declaration of Independence, brought East Florida into the limelight. The commission sought to "recall Florida's heritage" and to "examine the role played by Florida in the years leading up to the Revolution and during the American Revolution."[5] The commission published and disseminated specialized monographs, school pamphlets, and rare out-of-print facsimiles on Florida in the American Revolution. Five symposia were organized and held annually 1972–1976 on Florida's state university campuses. Scholars were invited to investigate aspects of the social, economic, intellectual, and political events surrounding eighteenth-century Florida. Five volumes published by the University Presses of Florida emerged from these conferences. After the conclusion of Florida's bicentennial celebrations, East Florida in the American Revolution again fell into obscurity. Since then, apart from a few scattered publications, no detailed source has paid sole attention to East Florida in the American Revolution.

WINSTON CHURCHILL CALLED THE Seven Years' War the first true world war. The North American theater of the Seven Years' War is also referred to as the Great War for the Empire, which was fought primarily between New France and British North America. Spain entered the war in 1762. Hostilities came to an end with the Treaty of Paris, signed on February 10, 1763. This treaty is sometimes called the Peace of Paris since Paris was where the peace negotiations took place.[6] Because of her participation in the Seven Years' War, Spain exchanged her Florida territory, *La Florida*, for Britain's Havana, Cuba, on November 3 during the 1762 peace preliminaries.[7] Havana was an important Spanish port in the Caribbean that was lost to the British during the Seven Years' War. This trade demonstrated Britain's resolve to fulfill its dreams of a continental empire rather than a commercial one.[8] The rationale for this decision stemmed from British opinion that North America's value as a market was more profitable than was sugar production in the West Indies.[9] This point is of considerable significance and demonstrates the value Britain placed on the North American colonies, especially considering how important sugar was in the world economy. According to Dr. Roger Smith, "In the eighteenth-century, sugar had the same impact on world economies as crude oil does today."[10] Indeed, European empires became dependent on sugar and even used the sugar trade to finance their global expansion.[11] As such, Article 20 of the 1763 Treaty of Paris ceded "Florida, with Fort St. Augustin, and the Bay of Pensacola, as well as all that Spain possesses on the continent of North America, to the East or to the South East of the river Mississippi."

Florida's transfer from Spain to Britain was not popular among British Parliamentary officials who were stunned by the deliberate loss of Havana. In their eyes, the trade-off of Havana for Florida was uneven. Many officials viewed Cuba as more valuable than Florida. In an address to the House of Commons, William Pitt declared that "Florida was no compensation for the Havannah." Havana "was an important conquest" and that since the city was taken, "all the Spanish treasures and riches in America, lay at [Great Britain's] mercy." According to Pitt, to exchange Cuba for Florida was an inadequate trade that ignored the principles of reciprocity.[12] Alderman Beckford compared Florida to a barren Bagshot Heath, a colony consisting of nothing but "pine barrens or sandy deserts."[13] In the end, two important arguments supporting Florida's acquisition won the day. First, Florida's possession would eliminate the Spanish threat to Georgia, and second, British ports in Florida would serve as bases for privateering in future wars with France.[14]

At the time of *La Florida*'s acquisition, the Proclamation of 1763 organized Florida's colonization. Since the proclamation prohibited westward expansion over the Appalachian Mountains, British leaders envisioned channeling settlement away from the west toward Canada and Florida.[15] The brainchild of this idea to resettle westward colonists in Canada and Florida came from Henry Ellis in a paper he presented before the Board of Trade, "Hints Relative to the Division and Government of the Conquered and newly acquired countries in America."[16] At length, in the aftermath of the French and Indian War, British leadership envisioned the regulated westward expansion of American settlers. British leaders sought to regulate westward settlement for a few reasons. They believed that unrestricted westward expansion would prove costly in the need to administer newly acquired territories; they feared that unrestricted expansion would produce ungovernable colonies who would, in time, desire to split with Great Britain; and, most importantly, they sought to avoid a war with the Native Americans who were promised the protection of their land under the British government from further white encroachments after Pontiac's Rebellion.[17]

Speaking to East Florida's relevance, Benjamin Franklin considered the colony in his diplomatic strategy. Sometime between September 26 and October 25, 1776, Franklin drafted what he called "propositions for peace with Great Britain." Among his numerous propositions, Franklin sought to purchase East and West Florida for the United States, promising to pay for that territory in the future.[18] Franklin's notes do not say exactly how much the United States was willing to pay, nor do they tell how many years it would take the United States to pay the debt in full. He may have deliberately left these sections blank and open to negotiation. Franklin's consideration of East Florida in his propositions to Britain reveal East Florida's presence in his mind. Franklin's consideration of East Florida, albeit however minor, points to just one aspect of that province's connection to the American Revolution. In the end, Franklin's propositions for acquiring Florida for the United States never reached Congress.

THIS BOOK OFFERS AN accessible and detailed narrative of East Florida during the American Revolution, with consideration given to the province's social, economic, political, and military history. Fundamentally, the narrative revolves around conflict. By placing center-stage the major events of East Florida in the American War of Independence, this work draws attention to East Florida's connection to and significance in that conflict.

1

British East Florida

Naturalist and explorer William Bartram traveled through East Florida in 1774 observing the terrain, flora and fauna, and people and later documenting what he witnessed in a famous book, popularly called *Bartram's Travels*. He described Amelia Island in northeast Florida as reedy, grassy, and very fertile, its inlets, sounds, and coasts abounding with a wide variety of fish. Rivers in eighteenth-century Florida afforded travelers effective inland transportation through the region's dense forests and swamplands. Trees were draped with Spanish moss. Birds, animals, and reptiles were varied and abundant. He also remarked on East Florida's indigenous population. While traveling down the St. Johns River, he stumbled across an Indian settlement consisting of eight to ten dwellings. The occupants were, he said, civil, happy, and naked.[1]

Overall, Bartram's account reveals that eighteenth-century East Florida was beautiful but wild. For Europeans, here as in similar frontier colonies, life in East Florida could be brutal. On one occasion, a party of drunken British soldiers from the St. Augustine garrison marched the wife of a local tavern owner at bayonet point to their fort, where they raped her. They brought her back to her tavern and forced her and her husband to serve them ale. Sometime later, one of the soldiers was charged with

MICO CHLUCCO the LONG WARIOR or KING of the SIMINOLES

TRAVELS
THROUGH
NORTH & SOUTH CAROLINA,
GEORGIA,
EAST & WEST FLORIDA,
THE CHEROKEE COUNTRY, THE EXTENSIVE TERRITORIES OF THE MUSCOGULGES, OR CREEK CONFEDERACY, AND THE COUNTRY OF THE CHACTAWS;
CONTAINING
AN ACCOUNT OF THE SOIL AND NATURAL PRODUCTIONS OF THOSE REGIONS, TOGETHER WITH OBSERVATIONS ON THE MANNERS OF THE INDIANS.
EMBELLISHED WITH COPPER-PLATES.

BY WILLIAM BARTRAM.

PHILADELPHIA:
PRINTED BY JAMES & JOHNSON.
M,DCC,XCI.

Title page of Bartram's Travels *(State Archives of Florida).*

sexual assault. He then blew his brains out. Angered over the loss of their comrade, belligerent soldiers blamed the tavernkeeping couple and destroyed the tavern. British colonial officials searched in vain for the culprits. The British garrison commander refused to cooperate in the investigation lest he lose control of his troops. In an unrelated incident, an angry customer shot and robbed the owner of an East Florida inn. On another occasion, a drunken confrontation between an Indian chief's son and a British soldier resulted in the Indian's death after a bayonet was thrust into his groin.[2]

East Florida began as a far-flung outpost in the British Empire. After Spain relinquished the territory, British troops took possession of East Florida at the colony's capital, St. Augustine, on July 20, 1763. General Jeffrey Amherst dispatched Lieutenant Colonel James Robertson to tour and inspect St. Augustine. Colonel Robertson arrived on September 8, 1763, and reported that the city was a struggling settlement, overgrown by weeds, and unproductive of any supplies except fish. The Proclamation of October 7, 1763, established the province's boundaries—from the Gulf of Mexico and Apalachicola River on the west, north from the Apalachicola to a point where the "Chatahouchee and Flint rivers meet," east to the source of the St. Marys River, and then the course of the St. Marys River to the Atlantic Ocean and the Gulf of Florida on the east and south, including all islands within six leagues of the coast. [3] Between August 1763 and January 1764, 3,063 Spanish subjects from 542 households departed East Florida, the last leaving with the colony's Spanish governor, Melchor Feliu, on January 21, 1764.[4] Only three Spanish families chose to remain behind and live under British jurisdiction.[5]

James Grant, a Scot who hailed from Ballindalloch Castle, was appointed the first British governor of East Florida. Grant had joined the British army in 1741 and fought in the French and Indian War, serving under Brigadier General John Forbes in the campaign to capture Fort Duquesne from the French. In 1758, Grant launched an unsuccessful attack against the fort and was captured by the French and imprisoned in Montreal. After his release, Grant later fought the Cherokees in the Anglo-Cherokee War. On June 24, 1763, Grant petitioned London for appointment as royal governor of West Florida. His application drew some interest among government officials, who instead offered him the governorship of East Florida (West

Portrait of General James Grant, first governor of East Florida (State Archives of Florida).

Florida's governorship went to George Johnstone). Governor Grant arrived in East Florida aboard the sloop *Ferret* on August 29, 1764.[6] He then took two months to set up a civil government, and by October 31, 1764, East Florida boasted a council, its civil governing body, with members appointed by the governor.[7] The council's early tasks included the implementation of police, safety, and sanitation regulations.[8]

During its early years, East Florida's approximately three thousand inhabitants were concentrated in the northeast corner of the colony between the St. Johns River and the Atlantic coast. Two-thirds of the population resided in St. Augustine, then East Florida's only seaport.[9] St. Augustine proper boasted three hundred to four hundred houses, mostly of typical Spanish masonry construction,[10] usually one or two stories tall, and with coquina or tabby walls, a tabby floor, cypress shingle roofs, and without chimneys. Their walls were usually plastered with a coat of whitewash but sometimes painted ocher, brown, green, or red. Windows faced east or west to catch the prevailing breezes. Wooden shutters and braziers provided warmth on cold days.[11] The British added fireplaces to these structures and sometimes built wooden second stories for extra living space.[12] Balconies jutted over the streets while stone or wooden fences masked private courtyards whose gardens contained herbs, flowers, grape arbors, vegetables, and citrus trees.[13] Every family in St. Augustine was said to have at least one citrus tree.[14]

The colony's population was made up of small traders, artisans, government officials, and soldiers. St. Augustine boasted a school, a bathing-house, a slaughtering pen, and a market, all maintained at the public's expense. The city's governmental buildings were all inherited from the Spanish.[15] The town plaza was surrounded by the most important edifices, including the incomplete bishop's house, the military guardhouse, the governor's palace, and the hospital. The plaza was the town's economic, political, and social center.[16] Rows of orange trees flanked it.[17]

St. Augustine had been protected since 1565, during the First Spanish Period, by wooden forts.[18] A 1668 pirate attack motivated Spanish authorities to provide a proper defense for the settlement. From a Spanish perspective, if St. Augustine fell, it threatened to upset shipping between Spain and the West Indies.[19] On November 18, 1670, Florida governor Manuel de Cendoya petitioned Marquess de Mancera, the viceroy of New Spain who was then residing in Mexico City, for finances to construct a stone fort at St. Augustine. Viceroy Marquess met with the general council of finance on December 16, 1670, to discuss this matter. In the end, the council, already aware of the recently established English settlement at Charleston, which challenged and threatened the Spanish presence in Florida, agreed to finance the fort's construction.[20] Work on the resulting Castillo de San Marcos began on October 2, 1672,[21] and was completed in 1695. Its walls, three feet thick and twenty-one feet high, were made of coquina, a pliable shell stone quarried in nearby Anastasia Island.[22] At the time of East Florida's British occupation, the Castillo boasted a ravelin and a bastion at each of its four corners. Earthworks supported by palm log palisades provided an additional line of defense.[23]

Historian Charles Loch Mowat said Spanish St. Augustine had the attributes of a garrison town.[24] Historian J. Leitch Wright Jr. said it resembled a walled medieval town. Recurring pirate, In-

Present-day photo of Castillo de San Marcos (State Archives of Florida).

dian, and English attacks motivated the Spanish government to invest further in the town's defenses.[25] In 1734, an earthen wall, reinforced with a wooden palisade and ten redoubts of earth or masonry, was erected to protect the town on three sides; Matanzas Bay guarded the fourth side.[26] In 1763, the Spanish added four entrenchment barriers, or "Lines," of earth and wood.[27] Three of the four protected against northern land approaches, the most likely attack by an English force.[28] The Cubo Line ran from the Castillo to the Sebastian River; the Hornwork Line was a half mile further north; and the Fort Mose Line was another mile and a half north.[29] The fourth, the Rosario Line, built in 1718, was a man-made barrier running south, along modern-day Cordova Street, from the Santo Domingo Redoubt for about a mile before turning east to Matanzas Bay.[30] Sharp dense yucca and prickly pear cactus covered the earthen mount, made high from earth excavated from a deep moat sitting directly in front of the earthen embankment.[31]

The Castillo de San Marcos still stands. After their takeover, the British renamed it Fort St. Mark, but the name reverted, and today the structure is known again as the Castillo de San Marcos or simply the Castillo.[32]

Throughout the British period, St. Augustine was a military station. In peace time, the colony boasted one infantry regiment, a company of artillerymen, and a civil branch of the military, which included a storekeeper, a surgeon, a blacksmith, a carpenter, one or two engineers, a fort adjutant, a barracks master, a chaplain, a commissary, and a "clerk of the survey and cheque." The regiment usually consisted of two hundred men who were mostly stationed at the capital while smaller detachments maintained the colony's outposts at New Smyrna, Apalache, Mosa, Anastasia Island, Matanzas, and Picolata. One company from East Florida was also stationed at New Providence in the Bahamas.[33]

During the American Revolution, Fort St. Mark was used as a prison.[34] Three South Carolinian signers of the Declaration of Independence, Arthur Middleton, Thomas Heyward Jr., and Edward Rutledge, were captured at Charleston in May 1780 and imprisoned in St. Augustine.[35] Another prominent rebel prisoner was Christopher Gadsden.[36] A prominent leader of the South Carolina patriot movement during the Imperial Crisis and later Revolutionary War, Gadsden was elected in 1762 to the South Carolina House of Assembly. He was a leader of the Sons of Liberty when the group hung the effigy of a stamp collector in October 1765. In July 1774, he attended the First Continental Congress as a South Carolina delegate. He was also a delegate of the Second Continental Congress and in 1776 became an officer in the Continental Army. When East Florida governor Patrick Tonyn offered Gadsden parole, he stubbornly refused, preferring to remain imprisoned in Fort St. Mark. Gadsden was released on July 17, 1781, after which he was shipped off to Philadelphia.[37]

French prisoners were also kept at Fort St. Mark, which quickly reached capacity. To remedy this situation, prisoners were paroled and kept in private houses in St. Augustine.[38] Wealthy prisoners rented rooms in town and bought food at the market. Less fortunate prisoners found shelter wherever they could and subsisted off government rations. Upon the prisoner's parole,

Governor Tonyn warned British residents not to have "friendly intercourse" with the prisoners. Parolees were ordered to report to the statehouse twice a day. The prisoners were generally left alone, but on rare occasions drunk loyalists harassed them. Once, pumpkins and oranges were pelted at the houses where prisoners stayed. On a separate occasion, musicians on the street mockingly played "Yankee Doodle."[39] Prisoners were not kept long at St. Augustine. They were hurriedly exchanged or sent to the West Indies. Estimates claim that roughly two thousand prisoners were kept in East Florida during the American Revolutionary War.[40]

Prisoners of war in East Florida generally fared well, though some better than others. A French prisoner, the Marquis de Bretigny, was captured off the coast of Charleston, brought to St. Augustine, and incarcerated in the Castillo's dungeon. Guards withheld his food and water. At one point, the guards threw a sickly Minorcan woman into his cell. She died and her body was left in the cell for thirty-six hours. After many unsuccessful attempts, Bretigny eventually escaped East Florida disguised as a seaman.[41] While some cases of cruelty and harassment are found in the documented prisoner of war experiences in St. Augustine, it was far better to be imprisoned there than anywhere else. Further north, the British commonly housed captured American prisoners of war in unsanitary and overcrowded prison ships. These prisoners were malnourished and frequently succumbed to disease from the cruel living conditions.

IMMEDIATELY UPON INHERITING EAST Florida's governorship, Grant needed to set up a functioning civil government.

To accomplish that end, Grant was given the power to build East Florida's government from the ground up. Such power was limited by Parliament's instructions, demanding that Grant remain in regular communication with officials in Whitehall. Grant was also forced to share power with East Florida's council. In addition to the council, a host of officials assisted Grant in administering East Florida. These officials were appointed by the governor on temporary terms of service. Their appointment required the home government's confirmation and approval. An annual Parliamentary grant paid their salaries. These officials included the chief justice, the attorney general, the register, the provost martial, the receiver general of the quit rents, two schoolmasters, two clergymen, the secretary and clerk of the council, the surveyor general, the crown agent, the pilot, a coroner, the man in charge of the fire engine, the messenger of the council, the clerk of the market, cryer of the courts, clerk of the public accounts, keeper of the Indian presents, and the public vendue master; customs officials and naval officers belonged in a separate category. The governor could suspend any official so long as he had the council's consent.[42] In April 1771, East Florida's Court of Vice Admiralty was created.[43] This branch of government wielded judicial authority and oversaw maritime court cases.

Apart from domestic concerns, Grant also took on other responsibilities. For one, he had to remain vigilant against Spain, who claimed territory in Central America, South America, New Orleans, the North American Southwest, and parts of the West Indies. Indeed, British leaders believed the Spaniards sought to reclaim Florida. In addition to the Spanish threat,

Grant maintained diplomatic ties with Florida's indigenous population. In fact, several Indian villages and settlements were situated close to St. Augustine. Most East Florida Indians were Seminole.[44] Cowkeeper was the principal Seminole chief.[45] During the Revolutionary War, the Seminoles fought for the British. Grant's relationship with East Florida's Indians was incredibly involved. Between 1762 and 1779, John Stuart, the superintendent of Indian affairs in the southern district, was simultaneously engaged in negotiating the Indian boundary line south of Virginia and maintaining relations with the Choctaws, Chickasaws, Cherokees, and Creeks—tribes who primarily did not occupy lands in or around East Florida.[46] With all Stuart's energies occupied on western Indian diplomacy, Grant was left to his own devices in managing East Florida's Indian affairs. Grant made it a point to treat the Indians justly and fairly. The Indian trade was thus regulated to ensure that no disputes arose out of bad deals.[47] Several trading posts were erected around East Florida for the purposes of conducting trade with the Indians.[48] If trade disputes flared, British officials feared they could quickly turn violent and produce an Indian war. Indian wars were a costly endeavor. Luckily, British East Florida avoided any such war. Grant's policy of fairness toward the Indians produced beneficial results. In effect, good relations flourished between East Florida and her neighboring Indian tribes. Peace prevailed despite the many times when that peace came into question. Grant's successful system of dealing with the Natives was employed by the subsequent East Florida governors who came after him.[49]

British colonial North American governments included a

governor and a two-chambered legislature consisting of an upper house, sometimes referred to as the council, and a lower house, sometimes known as the general assembly. Members of the lower house were made up of locally elected representatives, while the upper house comprised members appointed by the Crown.[50] Most of Britain's North American colonies had a general assembly. In essence, the lower house provided a voice for the people. During most of its existence, East Florida did not have a general assembly. Between the late seventeenth century and throughout most of the eighteenth century leading up to the American Revolutionary War, the power and influence of colonial North America's lower houses grew. During that time, the general assembly gradually took control of the financial power of their respective provinces. According to Jack P. Greene, "although each of the lower houses developed independently," their paths of increasing authority all reached the same conclusion: the desire for representation in British Parliament.[51] This growth of the lower assemblies' power contributed to American colonial discontent, which ultimately culminated in the Imperial Crisis and later Revolutionary War. East Florida's first general assembly met in 1781, eighteen years after the colony became an official British province. Because East Florida boasted no lower house until 1781, its council exercised legislative power. In addition to legislative matters, the council shared East Florida's executive and judicial powers with the governor. Since the governor elected East Florida's council, much authority in that province was concentrated in the hands of a few elite government officials. Without an elected assembly, East Florida's government resembled an aristocracy.

It is up to speculation to discover the reason why East Florida took so long in developing its lower house. It is possible that James Grant preferred not to have one. Charles Mowat claims that Grant prolonged the establishment of a lower house after he became aware of the growing anti-British movement in the northern colonies.[52]

In conjunction with creating a civil government and administering East Florida's external affairs, Grant was also concerned with his province's growth. According to David Chesnutt, Grant sought to make East Florida in South Carolina's model, a successful plantation colony.[53] After 1763, publicity and the dissemination of information enhancing East Florida's attractivity attempted to draw investors and settlers to that province.[54] According to James Raab, plans for East Florida's development rested heavily on persuading skilled planters from other parts of the British Empire to relocate to East Florida.[55] Governor Grant recommended East Florida plantations employ African Americans because he believed white planters were not dependable for a Florida plantation's long-term profitability.[56] East Florida's literal settlement was accomplished through a royal land policy and the contributions of East Florida's surveyor general, William Gerrard De Brahm, who prepared numerous detailed maps of East Florida from 1765 to 1771.[57]

Concerning East Florida's settlement, the Proclamation of 1763 outlined a royal land policy that disbursed land by two primary means. The first method awarded land grants for the establishment of townships, allotting twenty thousand acres to persons who would self-fund the colonization of the Florida wilderness alongside "a proper number of Protestant families."[58] The second method by which a person could receive Florida land was through land grant applications submitted to the governor and council. Between five colonies who granted royal land grants within their province's boundaries—New York, East and West Florida, Nova Scotia, and Quebec—the Privy Council received the most applications for East Florida land. Between 1764 and 1770, the Privy Council issued 227 orders for land grants in East Florida.[59] Independently wealthy gentlemen, aristocrats, prominent government officials such as Lord Dartmouth and Lord Townshend, and members of the East Florida Society who met at the Shakespeare Head Tavern in Covent Garden, all sought East Florida land.[60] Based on the relatively large amount of land grants issued to prospective investors and considering all of the interest East Florida received in London, East Florida should have grown faster than it did. Unfortunately, most of the issued land grants were purchased by wealthy English gentlemen seeking to enlarge their holdings through the acquisition of massive tracts of East Florida land. These gentlemen had no intention of cultivating their Florida estates by their own hand. Some of these wealthy men hired agents to go to Florida and establish a plantation in their stead, and that is if anyone was sent at all.[61] All things considered, many East Florida land grants were left uncultivated by absentee owners.

Some of the more noteworthy plantations born out of East Florida's British colonial period include Dr. Andrew Turnbull's New Smyrna colony; the Earl of Egmont's plantation on Amelia Island; Richard Oswald's plantation on the Tomoka River; and John Moultrie's plantation, "Bella Vista," situated four miles from St. Augustine on the Matanzas River.[62] This is to say nothing of Governor Grant's plantation, which he used as a model of a successful plantation to encourage investors to establish their own settlements in East Florida.[63] Despite the success of some settlements, many East Florida plantations failed.[64] Absentee planters were the norm and not the exception during British East Florida's development. While it is evident that land grants were issued, not many were cultivated. Lieutenant Governor John Moultrie wrote, "Many hundred thousand acres of [East Florida's] best land lies granted to grantees at home [and remains] but uncultivated."[65] Of the 227 applications for East Florida land grants submitted between 1764 and 1774, only 114 grants were issued. Of those 114 grants, only 16 had been settled. British East Florida settlement records are misleading when trying to capture a comprehensive and definitive snapshot of East Florida's development. They do not consider the squatters, frontiersmen, and individual land purchases that existed in that province's undocumented settlement.[66]

Taken together, historian Bernard Bailyn claims that East Florida's settlement was a failure.[67] According to historian Daniel Schafer, he believes that Bailyn did not consider the local St. Augustine residents who operated successful plantations.[68] Whatever conclusions are drawn regarding the success, or lack thereof, of East Florida's settlement, one thing is certain: it experienced sluggish development when that province's evolution is compared to the ambitions and visions of those who encouraged its rapid growth. The uncultivated land left untouched by East Florida's absentee planters discouraged fresh investors and prospectors from settling the region. Despite their role in East

Florida's slow development, the absentee planters were not the sole reason for East Florida's retarded growth. No. Four more significant reasons speak to East Florida's hindered growth. They included the need for purchasers to apply for land grants in person to the council in St. Augustine, preventing many speculators from obtaining land grants; the fees to purchase all the necessary documentation to support an official land grant were steep; the cost of living in East Florida was high;[69] and finally, the large quantities of uncultivated land purchased by eighteenth-century gentlemen across the Atlantic obstructed the ability of residents to settle East Florida land.

Notwithstanding East Florida's slow growth, not all development in that province was less than stellar. In 1765, planning and work for the king's road, extending from St. Augustine to Georgia, began.[70] The road was completed in 1775.[71] A lack of available finances coupled with work delays prolonged the road's completion. The opening of the king's road brought East Florida many settlers from the southern colonies, principally from Georgia and the Carolinas.[72] Another road extended from St. Augustine south to New Smyrna and yet another from Cowford, located at the present-day city of Jacksonville, to Amelia Island.[73] Two flatboat ferries, one situated on the St. Marys River and the other at the St. Johns River at Cowford, guided travelers across the water.[74] Economically, East Florida exported valuable resources to Great Britain. Indigo proved to be the most important contribution to the empire's mercantile interests. In 1782, England imported 569,443 pounds of indigo. Of that number, Florida contributed 125,533 pounds.[75] In addition to indigo,

East Florida also exported sea island cotton, citrus fruits, rice, deerskins, cowskins, flour, honey, and pork.[76] According to historian Samuel P. Turner, the British adapted Spain's "economic model for short term survival" by exporting commodities that were easily acquired in East Florida.[77] Concerning the capital's development, renovations on some of St. Augustine's old Spanish buildings and improvements made to the Governor's House were all done under the British.[78] The Governor's House, a two-story coquina building with a balcony that commanded

Drawings of (top) the Governor's House in St. Augustine and (bottom) view from a window in the house of the harbor; both ca. 1764 (State Archives of Florida).

a view of the west side of St. Augustine's plaza, was the scene of many dinner parties and became a hub of social activity for the province.[79] Grant used these dinners to liven up the sometimes boring military town and to recruit wealthy planters to invest in East Florida land.[80] East Florida also offered opportunities for those willing to call the place home. Trained artisans were in short supply, and anyone skilled in almost any trade could do well for themselves.

During Grant's tenure as East Florida's governor, he helped Britain establish a working government in that province, a task he was forced to complete from scratch. On March 4, 1774, Lieutenant Colonel Patrick Tonyn officially replaced James Grant as governor of East Florida.[81] Not much is known about Tonyn's origins. He was born in Ireland in 1725. He was commissioned as an officer in the 6th Regiment of Dragoons at the age of nineteen. He fought in Germany during the Seven Years' War and became a lieutenant colonel in the 104th Regiment of Foot in 1761.[82] According to Daniel Schafer, Tonyn was "intolerant and short-tempered, [he] demanded strict deference to class and rank, and treated any questioning of his authority with a rigid military disdain."[83] He was inaugurated at St. Augustine on March 9, 1774. He was an unpopular governor. Upon his arrival in St. Augustine, residents pressed him to create a general assembly. Because of the civil unrest that gripped the northern colonies, Tonyn refused to establish a lower house. His refusal came at a bad time. By the occasion of his arrival, East Florida moaned for a general assembly. Tonyn's refusal to call together a lower house factionalized East Florida's political scene. Despite some political dissent, East Florida's loyalty never came

Painting of Patrick Tonyn, Governor of East Florida, ca. 1774 (State Archives of Florida).

into question during the Imperial Crisis and later Revolutionary War. Why was that the case? East Florida was commercially dependent on Great Britain and the southern English colonies. Evidence that speaks to East Florida's submission can be found after the implementation of the 1765 Stamp Act and 1773 Tea Act. No opposition to the taxes ever materialized in East Florida. Boasting to Lord Dartmouth about East Florida's loyalty in the wake of the 1773 Tea Act, Governor Tonyn suggested that East Florida be used to distribute tea to the rest of the southern colonies. St. Augustine tea, Tonyn boasted, would not be seized by the rebels.[84]

To retain her North American possessions, the British Crown incurred heavy debts from the French and Indian War. Residents of the British Isles endured steep taxes that were used to pay for the war effort. Meanwhile, North American colonists paid no taxes. After 1763, Parliament levied several taxes on her North American colonies to refill British coffers. After all, British ministers thought, it is only fair that the colonies share the financial burden of their own defense. Prior to 1763, salutary neglect witnessed the lax enforcement of British laws in North America. The provinces were largely left to their own devices. After 1763, Parliament's sudden enforcement of colonial regulation ushered in colonial discontent, eventually contributing to the anti-British movement. Dissatisfied colonists touted "no taxation without representation" due to their lack of representation in British Parliament. This period, between 1763 and 1775, is called the Imperial Crisis. In the wake of civil disorder in the north, East Florida remained unaffected by the anti-British movement. In fact, East Florida was quite submissive throughout that time. There are two reasons that explain why East Florida passively accepted Parliament's duties. First and foremost, Floridians benefitted from continent-wide taxes. These taxes appropriated money from the northern colonies to help pay for new barracks in St. Augustine. Secondly, East Florida ran a trade deficit from 1763 to 1775.[85] To ensure East Florida's survival, the British government subsidized that province.[86] Subsidies paid for East Florida's Indian gifts, defense, and government.[87] During the Revolutionary War, the British East Florida garrison relied on food imported from England and Ireland.[88]

Throughout the Revolutionary War, loyalists who were unfortunate enough to live in patriot-controlled regions endured brutal violence. Tories were beat, tarred and feathered, scalped, bullied, harassed, humiliated, and had their property confiscated. Some were killed. To escape the clutches of whatever ill fate the rebels had in store for them, loyalists flocked to East Florida. Consequently, East Florida's population quintupled from four thousand in 1775 to over seventeen thousand in 1783.[89] Most of these incoming refugees were concentrated in and around St. Augustine.[90] Abandoning their homes, loyalists desperately traveled to East Florida however they could. Some used Indian trails while others traveled by water.[91] The makeup of East Florida's loyalist community varied. Most came from Georgia and the Carolinas. Loyalist refugees were represented across the socioeconomic spectrum. Some were members of provincial council's or assemblies while others were wealthy Indian traders. Most, however, were farmers who came from humble backgrounds.[92]

At Parliament's behest, on November 1, 1775, Tonyn issued a proclamation offering refuge in East Florida for loyalists seeking to escape the rebellion.[93] To compensate them for their loyalty, East Florida's loyalist refugees received a fifty- to five-hundred-acre land grant on unoccupied land.[94] They were also given farming tools, for without them, Tonyn believed, "they could not be settled."[95] Tonyn subdivided vacant lands owned by absentee landowners and gave those lands to the refugees.[96] The governor also asked East Florida residents to permit refugees to settle some of their uncultivated land in exchange for rent or a portion of whatever crops the refugees managed to grow.[97] According to British thinking, if land was not made available to loyalist refugees, they would, in turn, be unable to rebuild their lives, forcing them to join the rebellion out of necessity. Many East Florida merchants and skilled artisans found plenty of work and profited handsomely off the refugees.[98]

African Americans also contributed to East Florida's population boom.[99] Surprised at how many African American slaves reached East Florida, Governor Tonyn wrote to Lord George Germain in 1776, asserting that the need for an East Florida militia would keep "in awe the Negroes who multiply amazingly."[100] Slaves helped build East Florida's fortifications while free African Americans served in the province's navy. As a matter of fact, African Americans made up two-thirds of some British vessels' crew. Many African Americans were multilingual, having the ability to speak English, French, and multiple African dialects. African Americans who fought for the British and impressed their superiors were given expensive clothing and time off. During the Revolutionary War, African Americans, free and slave alike, made up 15 percent of East Florida's fighting force.[101] Unlike freedom deals secured in Virginia between African bondsmen and British officials, slaves who served in the East Florida militia were not promised freedom in exchange for their services.[102] Skilled African Americans engaged in carpentry, blacksmithing, tanning, and jobs at sea. Free African Americans wore a silver armband while enslaved African Americans wore a heart-shaped badge. East Florida's African American population even founded their own Baptist congregation and paid for their own minister.[103]

When news of the Declaration of Independence reached St. Augustine, residents burned effigies of Samuel Adams and John Hancock.[104] Shortly after Tonyn's arrival in East Florida, the Continental Congress approved sending East Florida a letter, inviting them to join the rebellion and approve the resolutions passed by Congress.[105] Ultimately, East Florida never received the invitation and thus did not participate in the First or Second Continental Congress.[106] Even if East Florida received the invitation, it is highly unlikely that they would have responded. Indeed, no anti-British political party existed south of the Florida-Georgia border. No doubt, East Florida's lack of a general assembly contributed to that province's loyalty. In fact, during the Revolutionary War, East Florida was the only colony in British America, not including Quebec, without a lower house. While the presence of standing armies in North America after the French and Indian War upset northern colonists, redcoats were a welcome sight in Florida. In East Florida especially, British soldiers were needed for defense. They protected inhabitants from Spaniards and Native Americans. In the northern colonies, colonial militias afforded a reliable means of defense against Indian raids—those provinces did not necessarily need British regulars. On the other hand, East Florida's population could not support an efficient militia capable of defending the entire province.[107]

In spite of the fact that East Florida was an unabashedly loyal province, not everyone in that colony was a trusted king's friend. The Minorcans at New Smyrna endured cruel treatment at the hands of their overseers.[108] Because of their struggles, many East Florida residents suspected they would join the rebels if the right opportunity presented itself.[109] Two men, John and Francis Caine, were actually apprehended by British East Florida authorities after they were caught communicating with Georgia rebels. Major Mark Prevost was even caught sending letters to his French father-in-law who just so happened to be a prominent agent of Charles Gravier, Comte de Vergennes, French foreign minister during the American Revolution.[110] While Major Prevost participated in East Florida's defense on more than one occasion, his connection to the French raised some suspicions. In East Florida's civil government, Tonyn claimed that Andrew Turnbull and William Drayton were rebels and traitors who believed "Lord North would answer [for the Revolutionary War] with his head."[111] This accusation stemmed from the governor's quarrel with the two men. No evidence ever surfaced to condemn their alleged rebel sympathies, and it is highly likely Tonyn only branded them as such to bring about their end.

As East Florida's loyalist population boomed, that province simultaneously experienced a trade boom. The Revolutionary War's coming stimulated East Florida's economy. Because of the civil unrest in the rebellious thirteen colonies, Parliament banned all British provinces not engaged in rebellion from trading with the rebels. This spelled trouble for the empire's West Indies colonists who relied on commerce with Britain's mainland North American colonies.[112] Prior to the Revolutionary War, the British West Indies imported food and lumber, among other goods, from Britain's North American provinces.[113] In exchange, North American colonies received tropical commodities, bills of exchange, specie, and slaves.[114] The American Revolution's commencement disrupted the trade relationship between the West Indies and the original thirteen colonies. In consequence, East and West Florida sourced the West Indies' demand for raw materials. East Florida filled that demand by producing timber, barrel staves, cattle, naval stores, and corn, which were also, in addition to appeasing the West Indies' need for resources, used to feed the royal army.[115] While East Florida's economy improved in some areas, it hurt in others. On May 17, 1775, the Continental Congress placed an embargo on East Florida.[116] The embargo hurt East Florida's economy, especially considering how East Florida relied heavily on commerce with Charleston, Frederica, and Savannah.[117]

By 1775, Native American affairs increased in importance. Loyalist Indian traders were forced to use Florida as a base of trading operations with southern Indians or risk losing their business. Luckily for the East Floridians, the Seminoles remained loyal to Britain. Their allegiance to the Crown wavered, however, during the early stages of the Revolution when Whig overtures attempted to entice the Indians into joining the rebellion.[118] In the end, Florida Indians were well aware of Georgian land appetites, and for that reason they refused to side with the rebels.[119]

Planning for the upcoming war, London officials viewed East Florida as a base of operations from where they could launch a military offensive against the southern colonies.[120] Because of East Florida's steadfast loyalty, the commander-in-chief of British America, General Thomas Gage, diverted regulars away from Florida and sent them to other provinces that were in more urgent need of men.[121] In July and September 1775, two detachments of the 14th Regiment were dispatched from East Florida to Williamsburg, Virginia.[122] The 14th Regiment would go on to fight in the Battle of Great Bridge.[123] After the 14th Regiment's departure, East Florida's force dropped to twenty-four officers, ninety-eight enlisted men, and a company of artillerymen. On top of this force, twenty-three additional men were spread out around that province's various outposts located at New Smyrna, the Anastasia watchtower, Cowford, Matanzas Inlet, and the St. Johns River.[124] By October 1775, only thirty-five men were fit for duty in St. Augustine.[125]

Rumors of East Florida's invasion from the Carolinas alarmed Tonyn.[126] Assessing East Florida's defenses, Tonyn concluded that they were inadequate. To improve his province's defensibility, Tonyn decided to destroy the remains of Fort Mose, an unoccupied fort situated two miles north of St. Augustine, so that the rebels could not use it. He also repaired the Castillo de San Marcos.[127] Despite all these improvements, Tonyn could not prevent two incidents that damaged the strength of that colony. In July 1775, rebels seized the merchant vessel *Phillipa* off the Georgia coast. The *Phillipa* carried ammunition intended for the St. Augustine garrison.[128] Its capture robbed East Florida of much needed ammunition. In August 1775, the South Carolina privateer *Commerce* captured the *Betsey*, captained by a man called Lofthouse.[129] Captain Lofthouse brought much needed powder for the East Florida garrison. Consequently, 26 rebels seized 111 barrels and 37 kegs of gunpowder. While the rebels plundered, ten British soldiers aboard the *Betsey* plotted to retake the ship. The raiders fled the scene after discovering the coup.[130] In response to the *Betsey*'s seizure, Tonyn posted a £200 bond for anyone who captured the rebel captain responsible for seizing Captain Lofthouse's stores.[131] To ensure that the pirates did not get away, Tonyn dispatched an officer and thirty soldiers of the 14th Regiment aboard the *Florida* to track down the *Commerce*. In the end, the rebels got away.[132]

During the winter of 1775, Tonyn gathered and organized the loyalist refugees, awaited reinforcements from Pensacola, and planned an assault against Georgia and South Carolina.[133] In an attempt to bolster East Florida's meager defenses, Indian Superintendent Stuart stationed fifty Indians to camp near St. Augustine over the winter.[134] Further north, on December 17, 1775, General Washington received a packet of stolen letters, informing him of East Florida's weakness and large supply of arms and ammunition.[135] After receiving this intelligence, Washington penned a letter to John Hancock. According to Washington: "Governor Tonyn's & Many other Letters from [St.] Augustine Shew the weakness of the place . . . of what vast Consequence it woud be for us, to possess ourselves of it, & the great quantity of Amunition Contained in the Fort [the Castillo de San Marcos]."[136] Considering all the options available to them, rebel leaders agreed to wait out the remainder of 1775 before engaging in official military operations against East Florida. Rebel aspirations sought to either make East Florida a fourteenth state or annex the colony to Georgia.[137] For the last couple weeks of 1775, East Florida remained quiet of any Revolutionary hostilities or activity.

II

Border Warfare and the First American Invasion of East Florida, 1776

On January 1, 1776, the Continental Congress resolved that "seizing and securing the barracks and castle of St. Augustine will greatly contribute to the safety of these colonies, therefore it is earnestly recommended to the colonies of South Carolina, North Carolina and Georgia to undertake the reduction of St. Augustine . . . [and that an] expedition be undertaken without delay."[1] Shortly after Congress's resolution, General George Washington appointed General Charles Lee to assume command of East Florida's invasion.[2] Accordingly, Lee was given command of 2,500 troops from Georgia, the Carolinas, and Virginia.[3] On the ground, Lee's operation progressed slowly. By mid-February he had made no move to assault East Florida. Due to his unenthusiastic performance, Lee was recalled to Charleston. In his stead, General Robert Howe assumed command of East Florida's invasion. Like Lee, East Florida's conquest lagged under Howe, who preferred to wait until Lee once again resumed command.[4]

At the start of 1776, Governor Tonyn bolstered East Florida's defenses, managed Indian diplomacy, and took care of incoming loyalist refugees. As far as East Florida's defenses were concerned, the St. Augustine garrison in 1776 was made up of the 14th, 16th, and 60th Regiments. The 60th Regiment arrived in East Florida in April 1776. Between 1777 and 1779, the 14th and 16th Regiments were dispatched to New York and Georgia, leaving only the 60th Regiment behind in East Florida. The 60th Regiment remained in East Florida until 1782. Command of His Majesty's East Florida troops fell to Colonel Augustine Prevost of the 60th Regiment. Colonel Prevost was promoted to brigadier general in April 1777. Several provincial and militia corps operated in conjunction with the regulars in East Florida. Three noteworthy provincial corps existed in and around East Florida during the Revolutionary War. They were the South Carolina Royalists, the Royal North Carolina Regiment, and the Scopholites (a body consisting of various South Carolina backcountry settlers). In February 1776, East Florida's council approved the formation of a militia.[5] In August 1776, Tonyn issued a proclamation summoning all East Florida inhabitants to the St. Augustine statehouse. On that day, Tonyn ordered East Florida's residents to form a militia. Lieutenant Governor John Moultrie was made the militia colonel. In total, Tonyn expected to raise eleven companies of men: two from the St. Johns River, four from St. Augustine, one from New Smyrna, and four companies consisting of men of African descent.[6] East Florida's militia were mostly tasked with police work and expected to perform patrol and guard duty.[7]

Of all the regiments assembled in East Florida during the British colonial period, the East Florida Rangers are the most noteworthy corps to come out of that province. As a matter of fact, they were present at every major engagement of the

American Revolution in East Florida. Raised in 1776, the East Florida Rangers, sometimes called Brown's Rangers in honor of the corps commander, Thomas Brown, recruited locals and loyalist refugees alike from the southern colonies.[8] The Rangers were organized into four companies. Men enlisted for three years. They were given clothing, provisions, and pay, but were required to provide their own horses.[9] Armed with rifles, Rangers typically wore hunting shirts.[10] Rangers were both black and white men.[11] They gathered intelligence, drove cattle, foraged, scouted, cooperated with Indians, and protected outlying settlements.[12] Since the unit's conception, contention between Colonel Prevost and Governor Tonyn existed over who com-

Portrait of Lieutenant Governor John Moultrie, ca. 1771 (State Archives of Florida).

manded the Rangers.[13] The East Florida Rangers answered to the colony's governor and not its military commander, a fact Prevost profoundly disliked.[14]

Before moving on, some attention must be paid to Thomas Brown, commander of the East Florida Rangers. Thomas Brown was born in the town of Whitby, England, on May 27, 1750. Brown aspired to become a gentleman planter in British North America's Georgia colony. In 1774 Brown recruited English colonists from Whitby and Scottish colonists from the Orkney Islands to emigrate with him and settle in Georgia. While in Georgia, Brown became a magistrate of his district and established the plantation of Brownsborough.[15] Unfortunately for Brown, his royal appointment and arrival to Georgia came at a very inopportune time. On August 2, 1775, a Sons of Liberty mob approached Brown at his home, demanding that he sign an association requiring his obedience to any measure adopted by Congress. Brown flatly refused to subscribe to the association. Turning angry, the mob ferociously descended upon him. The mob grabbed Brown and tied him to a tree, placing burning pieces of firewood beneath his feet. Next, the mob unleashed a variety of different punishments on the man. He was scalped in three or four places; he was tarred and feathered, resulting in the loss of two of his toes; a strike to his head from a rifle butt fractured his skull; all the while, looters ransacked his house. Immediately after the attack, Brown was paraded around Augusta, Georgia, in a cart.[16] The following morning, Brown promised the rebel gang who abused him that he would support the American rebellion. Satisfied, the Sons of Liberty provided Brown with a horse and released him.[17]

After his suffering and subsequent humiliation, Brown could not walk properly for months. He also endured frequent headaches, which afflicted him for the rest of his life. Adding insult to injury, Revolutionary War veterans mockingly remembered Brown for his nickname "Burnfoot Brown." Brown left Georgia and reached East Florida in 1776, hungry for revenge against his assailants.[18]

In addition to regulars and provincial and militia foot soldiers, East Florida's navy and Native American allies constituted the other portion of that province's military muscle. Throughout the Revolutionary War, Tonyn encouraged privateering and even issued commissions and letters of marque.[19] As late as 1779 to 1783, British privateers used St. Augustine as a base of operations for attacking French, Spanish, and American ships.[20] During the invasion of 1776, however, East Florida's navy often acted defensively to protect that province's coasts and inland waterways from rebel attack, a tremendously important task. Indeed, rebel privateers harassed British shipping around East Florida whenever they could. British ships operating in East Florida's waters were regularly fired upon and sometimes seized.[21] In addition to defense, East Florida's navy raided Georgian and South Carolinian coasts while Tonyn's privateers plundered rebel ships for supplies.[22] All vessels in East Florida waters that were not Royal Navy ships were searched.[23] East Florida's navy vessels included the *Cherokee*, *Lively*, *Haven*, *Otter*, *St. John*, *St. Lawrence*, *Hinchinbrook*, *Florida*, *Rebecca*, *Meredith*, *Hawke*, *Germaine*, *Dreadnought*, *Thunderer*, and the *Governor Tonyn*.[24]

Concerning Native American military might, there were few

Indians in East Florida, comparatively speaking, at the Revolution's onset.[25] In 1774, Wilbur Siebert claims that there were roughly two thousand Indians in East Florida. Compare that to West Florida, which contained fifteen thousand warriors between the Creek, Choctaw, and Cherokee nations.[26] From December 6 to December 8, 1775, British East Florida officials and Florida Indians met at a diplomatic congress at Cowford.[27] This meeting solidified an Indian-British alliance that lasted throughout the war.[28] The Natives in attendance were given gifts of beef, firearms, gunpowder, potatoes, rum, and various manufactured trinkets. In return, Tonyn received a tobacco pipe, eagle tails, and deerskins.[29] The British loathed Indian gift-giving, especially considering how costly that practice was. Yet, despite their opposition to gift-giving, it was necessary in order to keep the Native Americans from siding with the rebels.[30] Whatever personal opinions British officials harbored toward provisioning East Florida's indigenous population, that endeavor effectively secured Indian loyalty. In effect, this critical meeting at Cowford brought East Florida's Native American population into the war. Under their alliance, Indians were asked to hunt close to East Florida's frontier—if any fighting broke out, Tonyn wanted them ready and available to fight.[31] Tonyn assured the Indians in 1776 that the rebels were more afraid of them than they were of "any European army."[32] In addition to their aforementioned uses, East Florida Natives also stole cattle and guarded plantations against Georgian raiding parties.[33]

In the first couple years of the war, fighting was mostly restricted to East Florida's northeast frontier along the Florida-Georgia border and in the space between the St. Marys and St.

Johns Rivers. At that time, numerous British outposts guarded Florida's northeast frontier. Wright's Fort, situated on the north side of the St. Marys River, was the main British base of operations in that region, the site of coordinating raids against Georgian settlements.[34] Raids against frontier settlements residing around the East Florida–Georgia border occurred as early as 1775. Patriots burned British plantations, decimated British crops, and made away with British slaves and cattle.[35] In turn, the British repaid this kindness by burning Georgian plantations, decimating Georgian crops, and making away with Georgian slaves and cattle. In 1776, patriot raids intensified along East Florida's northern frontier.

While General Robert Howe awaited General Charles Lee's return, Georgia rebels brought the Revolutionary War to East Florida. In May, Georgia's Council of Safety authorized Captain William McIntosh and his "Troop of Horse" to seize Wright's Fort, proceed to the St. Marys River, capture any disaffected men, black or white, and secure any provisions or armaments they found. Additionally, McIntosh was ordered to seize any vessels on the St. Marys River and capture their contents; rustle any cattle he came upon—especially those owned by David Anderson; and construct log forts on the Altamaha and St. Marys Rivers.[36] These orders reveal the Georgian strategy: acquire prisoners, armaments, supplies, and livestock, and garrison strategic positions. The patriots' desired raiding targets reveal insights into the eighteenth-century reality of life on the East Florida–Georgia frontier. In the South, slaves were a plantation's lifeforce. Without them, a plantation's production ability dwindled or altogether came to an end. Gunpowder was a much needed commodity in East Florida and Georgia during the Revolutionary War. Georgia had no gunpowder source; much of what that state used came from privateer raids against incoming vessels to St. Augustine. The British also experienced gunpowder shortages and had to share what little stores they had with their Indian allies. Cattle was also in short supply on both sides. East Florida's population boom necessitated the consumption of large amounts of livestock while troop movements in southern Georgia interfered in that state's ability to produce optimal amounts of foodstuffs.[37]

Once Tonyn caught wind of Georgian objectives, he immediately dispatched a detachment of soldiers aboard the *St. John* to guard the St. Marys River crossing. The soldiers were ordered to arm the locals and instruct those with cattle to move them south of the St. Johns River.[38] The *St. John* was instructed to assume command of any vessels there, maintain communication lines with St. Augustine, and remain prepared to evacuate any soldiers in the area if overwhelmed by superior forces. British troops arrived at the St. Marys via the *St. John* on May 29, 1776, and dropped anchor. Upon their arrival, the soldiers established a camp on the south side of the river and a hospital on the north bank next to Wright's Fort. After establishing their base camp, British soldiers tracked down and caught up with the rebel raiders responsible for plundering numerous loyalist plantations. The raiders had taken prisoners and were making their way back to Georgia. A skirmish broke out just as the Georgians had crossed the river into their state. Both sides exchanged fire, resulting in the death of one British soldier from the 14th Regiment. Three Georgians were wounded, but not captured. Three Tory planters escaped during the engagement while later that night the British sent some men across the St. Marys to rescue those still in rebel captivity. In the days that followed, both the Georgians and East Floridians consolidated their respective frontiers. Each side fought for control of strategic points on the inland rivers. By this time, the British managed to effectively command the sea and waterways all the way to the St. Marys River.[39] Additionally, the British constructed Fort Tonyn twenty-five miles upstream on the St. Marys River next to the ferry and cow ford.[40] At the same time, the Georgians repaired old forts and fortified the port town of Sunbury. In June, Tonyn sent cattle hunters to the St. Marys border.[41] With the arrival of fresh reinforcements in St. Augustine, Tonyn began entertaining visions of Georgia's invasion from East Florida.

As border warfare ensued, Georgian raiders managed to penetrate deep into East Florida. Local residents sometimes aided the rebels. On July 1, 1776, a raiding party scoured as far south as the St. Johns River. They took a family and their thirty slaves prisoner. On July 11, the rebels renewed their offensive against Wright's Fort. At four o'clock in the afternoon, two musket shots issued from the fort indicated that it was under attack. A dozen men from the *St. John* went ashore only to discover that the fort's garrison had successfully repulsed the attack. Again, at six o'clock that same evening, the fort garrison fired two shots, signaling a renewed American offensive. This time, one hundred and twenty Georgians, a mix of infantry and cavalry, descended upon the hospital. By this time, men from the *St. John* attempted to land on shore in a canoe and assist their comrades. A troop of rebels hid in the marshes below the fort and ambushed the relief force. The canoe pulled away in time but not before a seaman was killed and another wounded. The American looting went on for a while. They did not leave until two o'clock in the morning. Amid the chaos, they stripped the dead and wounded, stole twenty slaves, and seized any provisions and bedding from the hospital they could carry. The men inside the hospital were safely brought to Wright's stockade fort before they could be taken prisoner. On July 13, the sick and wounded were evacuated from the area.[42]

In the summer of 1776, a troop of Georgian horsemen operated just north of the St. Marys River to protect Georgian cattle herds grazing in that region. They were probably stationed there due to Georgia's immense losses incurred from cattle rustling. By that summer, four thousand cattle were rustled across the St. Marys River into East Florida. To make matters worse, Tonyn's men captured six Georgian horsemen, prompting the rebels to relocate their base of operations north of the Satilla River. Around the same time, East Florida privateers raided South Carolina's coast.

By July 26, 1776, all British troops stationed on the St. Marys River fell ill, probably from prolonged exposure to the Florida-Georgia swamps. In that condition, the British were in no position to defend the East Florida border against Georgian forays. For that reason, two British ships, the *St. John* and the *Florida*, evacuated all the sick troops stationed on the St. Marys River, transferring them to Amelia Island. In consequence, the British position on the frontier became tenuous at best, and in August their position grew more alarming. In the beginning of that month, the border was manned by a meager force of seventy regulars, sixty-two armed slaves, twenty-three irregular riflemen, and the crews stationed aboard the *St. John*, the *Florida*, and the *Pompey*. On the morning of August 5, a small American navy made up of three water vessels, one schooner, a flatboat, and another vessel, sailed for East Florida. They intended to capture the *St. John* vessel, attack Wright's Fort, and seize slaves on Amelia Island. In total, the American force consisted of 260 men, a four-pounder, and six swivel guns. When Stephan Egan, an agent managing the Earl of Egmont's Amelia Island plantation, learned of the rebel invasion, he refused to leave Amelia Island, preferring instead to defend his employer's property with his life. On August 7, after American ships were sighted off the southern coast of Cumberland Island at four thirty in the morning, Egan changed his mind and abandoned Amelia Island with Egmont's slaves in tow. Meanwhile, the *St. John* opened fire on the American flotilla. Both sides fired their cannons at one another, but nothing came of this exchange. The Americans did, however, capture the British schooner *Pompey* while the *Florida* was blown up to ensure that the vessel remained out of rebel hands.[43] In the wake of British losses on the waters around the north end of Amelia Island, Crown forces evacuated their position there and withdrew south of the St. Johns River.

After the British withdrawal from Amelia Island, the rebels stood unopposed between the St. Johns and the St. Marys Rivers. Raiders burned Wright's Fort and decimated every plantation north of the St. Johns River. As a result, the St. Johns River became East Florida's new northern boundary. British soldiers of the 14th, 16th, and 60th Regiments remained on guard at Cowford.[44] Redcoats likely also manned Fort St. Nicholas, a fort near Cowford and located on the south side of the St. Johns River.[45] On August 15, Tonyn forbade anyone from crossing north of the St. Johns River and into the contested region between East Florida and Georgia without written permission from himself, the governor.[46] By then, East Florida was primed and ready for an invasion.

Further north, General Charles Lee harbored reservations about his army's ability to successfully besiege St. Augustine.[47] Finally, on July 31, after a long interim period in which nothing was done about the Georgian invasion of East Florida, Generals Lee and Howe finally marched their forces from Charleston to Savannah. They reached Savannah on August 7, 1776.[48] On August 19, General Lee consulted the Georgia Council of Safety to talk about East Florida's invasion. Lee asked the councilmen if they believed an invasion of East Florida was worthwhile considering the fact that his invasion force did not have the strength to support a siege of St. Augustine. Lee also asked that if the councilors believed East Florida's conquest was worthwhile, how did they plan on supporting the invasion force with transports and provisions? The council believed that if the settlers south and east of the St. Johns River were forced to abandon their plantations and flee into the Castillo de San Marcos, the Britons' want for supplies would be so great that the garrison would be forced to capitulate. Even if, the council asserted, the reduction of the St. Augustine castle could not come to fruition, an attempt to do so would diminish the threat of future raids from East Florida into southern Georgia.

Furthermore, an invasion of East Florida would reduce that province's strength and threaten her intercourse with the Native Americans, affecting British ability to provide gifts and unleash Native war parties against Georgia's backcountry settlers. Moreover, an invasion of East Florida would put an end to loyalist privateering along Georgia's coasts, destroying the East Floridians' ability to outfit naval raiding parties.[49]

Convinced and content with the information he received, Lee uttered no dissent against an invasion into East Florida. On August 18, all the troops intended for East Florida's conquest were stationed in Savannah. There was just one problem. On August 8, Lee was recalled to Philadelphia. Command of the continental troops in Georgia fell to General Robert Howe.[50] Once again unable to administer East Florida's invasion, Lee left that task to Colonel William Moultrie, the brother of East Florida's lieutenant governor, John Moultrie.[51] Lee hesitated in selecting Moultrie for command, mostly because of his familial connection to John. Colonel Moultrie eventually quieted Lee's fears and assumed command of the expedition. In short order, Moultrie discovered that the expedition was poorly provisioned. The men lacked shoes, no medical chest accompanied the expedition, wagons were in short supply, and dissension plagued campaign members from the start.[52] The reasons for dissension were many and probably due to a lack of appropriate provisioning or the environmental conditions the Americans would be forced to endure in order to begin attempts at taking St. Augustine from the British. In effect, marching through East Florida was no easy feat. Because the Okefenokee Swamp and Creek borderlands halted any southern advance across Georgia through most of the Florida interior, the only way any sizeable invasion force could enter East Florida was from the north on the king's road, a narrow corridor between swampland and the Atlantic coast.[53]

Two big rivers existed between East Florida's northern border and the city of St. Augustine. The Americans would need to ford these rivers at narrow points guarded by British garrisons. After fording the first river and penetrating East Florida, invaders would either have to march south on the king's road, exposing themselves to British musket fire, or they could slip away into the swamps and head south for forty miles through a landscape infested with quicksand, gnats, black bears, panthers, alligators, disease-carrying mosquitos, and poisonous snakes.[54] Apart from the deadly wildlife, there was virtually no fresh water awaiting the soldiers along their route.[55] Amid

Drawing by William Bartram of two alligators in the St. Johns River, ca. 1773 (State Archives of Florida).

these challenges, Florida's sweltering summer heat would likely incapacitate several expedition members. If the army made it through this part of the country, it would need to cross another large river, the St. Johns River, guarded by more British soldiers. If the Americans survived that, they would have to proceed south for another roughly forty miles through marshes and coastal flood plains if they wanted to avoid exposed marching on the king's road. By the time they neared St. Augustine, invaders would have to exit the swamps and endure cannon fire from the Cubo Line and the Castillo de San Marcos.[56] If the Americans were lucky, they would have some cannons themselves to return fire, assuming the artillery survived the long trek from Georgia through bogs, swamps, and marshes. Sure, the Americans could land artillery along the coast, but such a tactic would draw rebel ships into engagements with East Florida's navy. Approaching East Florida's capital, the Americans would then have to undertake a costly campaign, likely without artillery, in a protracted siege of St. Augustine. If this measure were even possible to accomplish without artillery, regular provisions would need to arrive through maintained and well-guarded supply lines. All the while, Brown's Rangers would utilize guerrilla tactics to wreak havoc on American supply lines. Until the defenders capitulated, which could take months, reinforcements and provisions could reach the British by sea. To prevent this, a rebel navy would need to blockade St. Augustine's port and hope that no hurricanes were scheduled for that year. This assertion assumes the rebels could even defeat East Florida's navy to allow for such a blockade to even occur. On balance, the undersupplied and undermanned American invasion force would need to confront these challenges in order to bring British East Florida to its knees.

Tonyn expected the rebel invasion and posted Seminole warriors on the west side of the St. Johns River. He then posted the *St. John* on the St. Johns River to protect the plantations there. On August 29, 1776, an American vessel seized the British ship *Clarissa* while it transported loyalist refugees to East Florida. On September 7, the British commanding officer stationed at Cowford on the St. Johns River reported that a large American force had been spotted on the north side of the river. A rebel raiding party was believed to have crossed the river, destroying plantations close to the river. Of the hundred-man British force stationed on the St. Johns River, one sergeant and five privates were captured in a minor engagement with the rebels. An Indian war party chased the Georgian raiders back to the St. Marys River.[57] As turmoil on East Florida's northern frontier threatened to supplant the British in East Florida, a similar threat emerged from the south near modern-day New Smyrna Beach. In the 1760s, Andrew Turnbull colonized East Florida's frontier with 1,400 settlers, mostly from Minorca, at a settlement called New Smyrna. Colonists at New Smyrna long hated their treatment at the hands of Turnbull and his overseers. These colonists were treated so badly most escaped New Smyrna and found refuge in St. Augustine during the Revolutionary War. East Florida loyalists eyed the New Smyrna colonists suspiciously on account of Turnbull's poor treatment of them. British East Florida officials feared New Smyrna's settlers would join the rebels if given the opportunity.[58]

By mid-September 1776, the rebel invasion of East Florida

failed completely. Upon General Lee's departure from Savannah, he took with him a sizeable portion of the invasion force. The remaining soldiers suffered immensely. Encamped along Georgia's southern rivers, these men sickened rapidly.[59] Without any medicine, fourteen to fifteen deaths occurred daily.[60] On top of sickness, men deserted to their backcountry homesteads to protect their families from rumors of Cherokee raids along the Georgia frontier.[61] Like that, rumors mixed with sickness brought the first American invasion of East Florida to an end. When all was said and done, the main body of Georgia's invasion force never made it further south than Sunbury, Georgia, only twenty-five miles south of Savannah.[62] The advance forces, however, made it as far south as the St. Johns River, but did not accomplish much past that point. Taken together, the 1776 invasion and East Florida–Georgia border war produced few casualties. Significant damage, however, was done to property. Every East Florida settlement north of the St. Johns River was destroyed. Crops were decimated. Loyalist victims of Georgian raids were forced to flee south of the St. Johns River if they wanted to remain relatively safe from further looting and capture. Despite these hardships East Florida's frontier population endured, St. Augustine was never threatened. In the aftermath of the failed rebel invasion, Georgia's military state was in a pathetic condition. That province could not provide its soldiers proper barracks, provisions, clothing, medicines, hospitals, tools, or tents. To make matters worse, nothing was being done to remedy these deplorable conditions.[63]

In late September 1776, British forces managed to take control of East Florida's northern border. Two vessels, the *Rebecca* and the *St. John*, patrolled the St. Johns River. A third unnamed vessel patrolled the St. Marys River.[64] On one of their patrols, the British captured a rebel brig on the St. Marys River. At the same time, the East Florida Rangers tore into Georgia. The Rangers stole cattle, plundered and burned plantations, and attacked Georgian settlers. The region between the Altamaha and St. Marys Rivers became the new no man's land between East Florida and Georgia—the place of raids and counter raids (this no man's land once existed between East Florida's St. Marys and St. Johns Rivers). For the rest of 1776, East Florida remained safe from any serious threat. While Tonyn entertained thoughts of invading Georgia and South Carolina, he did not have the manpower or finances to garrison captured territory in those regions. Unable to launch an invasion into Georgia, Tonyn focused on defense. He completed repairing East Florida's fortifications and successfully organized East Florida's militia. Ending the year on a high note, East Florida's economy thrived. Resources, especially lumber, were exported to the West Indies. According to Martha Searcy, "as many as forty to fifty vessels crowded St. Augustine's harbor [in 1776]."[65] In the end, despite rebel ambitions, by the end of 1776, East Florida remained firmly under British control.

III

The Battle of Thomas Creek and the Second American Invasion of East Florida, 1777

The state of Georgia was in poor condition at the start of 1777. All land south of the Altamaha River was unsafe for farming or grazing cattle. The state militia was underfunded and undersupplied. The British ship *Rebecca* captured a Georgian privateer. All settlements along Georgia's southern border were destroyed. Reports claimed that East Floridians took anywhere from three thousand to six thousand livestock from Georgia's southern frontier. British raids continued unabated against Georgia's southern frontier in 1777. The East Florida Rangers and their Native American allies championed these raiding efforts. Tonyn wanted to invade Georgia, given that state's inability to adequately defend her southern border. Colonel Augustine Prevost refused. Disagreements ensued until a famine loomed over East Florida. Between the refugee influx, delayed arrival of supplies, and the demand for Indian gifts, the province's needs overstimulated its reserves. Taking these realities into consideration, Prevost finally agreed to coordinate a joint military effort, combining his regulars with Tonyn's provincial forces. The objective? Rustle Georgian cattle.[1] Indian warriors would aid the rustlers. At the end of the day, Georgian livestock would provide for East Florida's needy population.

East Florida's invasion force assembled under the command of Lieutenant Colonel Lewis Fuser. The invasion force was made up of roughly four hundred Creek warriors, some artillery, one hundred East Florida Rangers (including Thomas Brown), and five hundred British regulars. In February, the army left St. Augustine on the king's road. Before moving into Georgia, Fuser's force constructed a fort at the St. Marys River, christened it Fort McIntosh, and left a fifty-man garrison.[2] Once news of the army's approach reached Georgia's frontier, settlers residing there abandoned their homesteads.[3] The little British army marched to the American-held Fort McIntosh, then situated on the Satilla River. Fort McIntosh stood on rising ground eighty yards from the Satilla River's north bank. It was a hundred feet square and contained a blockhouse in the center and a bastion on each corner. An advance party of Indians and Rangers reached the American fort on February 17 and opened fire.[4] The Americans retreated into the fort and returned fire. After both sides exchanged lead, the British ordered a ceasefire and Thomas Brown demanded the rebels lay down their arms. If they refused, he warned, his men would take no quarter. Captain Richard Winn, commander of Fort McIntosh, declined Brown's terms and the battle ensued once more. This was a bold move on Winn's part. Under his command, at the battle's onset he directed sixty Continental soldiers. Intense fighting reduced those numbers significantly. Because no physician was stationed at the fort, the wounded were forced to endure their injuries while the imminent threat of death loomed over their heads should Brown's

Indians or Rangers scale the walls. At dusk, Brown and his men withdrew. Overnight, the Rangers left sentries posted around the fort. Winn used this lapse in fighting to send a messenger to Fort Howe, an American fort situated roughly twenty-five miles away, requesting reinforcements. Unfortunately for Winn, Fort Howe's garrison was manned by only forty men and thus could not afford to offer any relief.[5]

That night, British regulars arrived under Lieutenant Colonel Fuser. Hostilities resumed at nine o'clock the next morning and lasted until three o'clock in the afternoon after which Fuser engaged Winn in negotiations, hoping the rebel officer would agree to capitulate and abandon the fort. Unaware that no reinforcements were coming from Fort Howe, Winn engaged Fuser in diplomatic discussion only to stall the attack long enough for relief to arrive. After talking for two hours, no reinforcements had come. At that moment Winn realized he was on his own. Running low on ammunition, the rebels had enough left to last one more day. Without outside help, Fort McIntosh could not sustain an extended attack. Left without options, Winn agreed to Fuser's terms. In return, he demanded only one thing: that Fuser and his regulars safely escort him and his men to Fort Howe. Winn demanded this point because he feared that once he and his men were far enough away from Fort McIntosh, they would be ambushed by Indians. The presence of British regulars, he reasoned, would protect them from that fate. Fuser refused this demand. In response, the rebel captain returned to the fort and prepared for another attack.[6]

The failed negotiations frustrated Lieutenant Colonel Fuser, who was anxious about operating so deep in enemy territory.

The unappealing prospect of waging a prolonged siege stared the British right in the face. Because Fuser was unaware of the rebels' dire situation, he once again called on Captain Winn to return to the bargaining table. Reluctantly, Fuser agreed to the rebel captain's demand for an escort across the Georgian frontier. Agreeing to these terms, the rebels surrendered Fort McIntosh on February 18. That night, the British escort gradually abandoned their task of accompanying the Americans to Fort Howe and returned to their camp. By ten o'clock, Captain Winn and his rebels were left unguarded. While alone in the woods, Winn feared an Indian attack. He was so frightened at that prospect, he ordered what was left of his men to hastily traverse thirty-five miles of Georgian woods and swamps. Their entire ordeal was spent looking over their shoulders and jumping at every snap of a twig or tree branch. Once under British occupation, Fort Mcintosh was burned on February 19. Fuser had his sights set on Fort Howe, but after engaging a sizeable rebel force at the Altamaha River, he was forced to turn around and head back to St. Augustine.[7] Fuser and his men returned triumphant to St. Augustine on March 5, 1777.[8] In total, the expedition managed to rustle two thousand Georgian livestock.[9] In consequence, East Florida was saved from a famine.

Georgia reeled from Fuser's invasion. In response to East Florida's offense, the Georgia Council of Safety talked of invading East Florida. Continental leaders like General Robert Howe did not believe Georgia could support or afford such an invasion. By March 1777, Georgia's backcountry was unstable. The state's soldiers deserted daily, and its regulars were in no considerable quantity.[10] Georgia was in such want for soldiers that some of her neighboring colonies to the north, like South Carolina and Virginia, had to send men to assist in her defense. Despite Howe's serious reservations about Georgia's inability to invade East Florida, George Washington wrote to him on March 17, 1777, delivering his opinion on the matter: "[St. Augustine] is an Object of considerable importance, & if it could be effected, would produce the most valuable and salutary consequences."[11] Washington similarly wrote to Jonathan Bryan, then serving on Georgia's Council of Safety, "If on consideration the measure [of invading East Florida] shall seem expedient & practicable, I flatter myself, that your State & that of South Carolina will cheerfully concur and give General Howe every aid necessary for the execution of it."[12] Washington's desire to invade East Florida stemmed largely from his need for flint and powder—supplies he believed East Florida contained in great quantities.[13] The commander-in-chief left the decision to invade East Florida with General Howe. Howe decided against committing his troops for the expedition against East Florida in 1777. Regardless of this fact, Georgian President Button Gwinnett invaded East Florida anyway.[14]

Colonel Samuel Elbert and Colonel John Baker were appointed leaders of Georgia's second invasion of East Florida.[15] Initially, General Lachlan McIntosh, a participant of the border war between East Florida and Georgia, was put in command of the expedition, but because of disputes regarding who would direct the overall invasion force, he was recalled in favor of Colonel Elbert.[16] While Georgia's leaders argued over who was in charge, southern Georgia was in a state of anarchy. As the invasion stalled throughout April due to political quarrels among Georgia's elite, Indians raided the Georgian frontier, killing indiscriminately. Once the Georgians finally agreed upon a commander for the expedition, the rebels invaded East Florida on two fronts. The first front, under Colonel Elbert, embarked a small navy of three galleys and transports laden with twenty cannons, two sloops, and four hundred Continental soldiers. This contingent left Sunbury by water on May 1, 1777.[17] Colonel Baker commanded the overland force, consisting of 109 mounted Georgia militia. The two commanders agreed to rendezvous at Sawpit Bluff, close to the St. Johns River. Colonel Baker arrived there first, on May 12. En route, he engaged in a brief skirmish with a band of Native Americans. Colonel Elbert, however, was nowhere to be found. Baker immediately set up camp and awaited Elbert's arrival. While they waited, a party of Native Americans entered Baker's camp and tried to make away with forty horses. In a frantic chase through the East Florida swamps, Baker's men recovered their horses, killing one Indian in the process. Two of Baker's men were wounded.[18]

After five days, Colonel Elbert was still nowhere to be found. Deciding his position was too exposed for an extended stay, Baker moved his men on May 16. He relocated upland to Thomas Creek, making camp there. That night, British Rangers located Baker's camp. In a coordinated effort, the East Florida Rangers, their Indian allies, and some British regulars under the command of Major Mark Prevost ambushed the Americans on May 17, 1777.[19] At ten o'clock in the morning, Brown, his Rangers, and some Indians shot at the Americans from behind trees.[20] The rebels were taken aback. After the first volley, half of Baker's force deserted into the swamps. The remaining force, including Baker himself, retreated, hoping to find more defensible ground. As they withdrew, the Americans ran headfirst into three columns of British regulars, all flashing fixed bayonets. The rebels were out of options. Ambushed and vastly outnumbered, they attempted to mount their horses and flee the scene, exposing themselves to intense British fire. At length, Colonel Baker and a few of his men managed to escape. The rest of Baker's force was taken prisoner. Altogether, eight Americans were killed, thirty-one were captured, and nine more were wounded. The Indians added to these casualties when, for whatever reason, they started killing survivors. Only sixteen were spared. Major Prevost had to intervene or else it is highly likely the rest would have been slaughtered.[21] No British soldiers or Native Americans were hurt in this engagement.

On May 18, a day after Colonel Baker's defeat at Thomas Creek, Colonel Elbert landed on the northwest end of Amelia Island.[22] According to Burton Barrs, Elbert landed "near the present [town of] Fernandina."[23] The rebels rounded up all the loyalist inhabitants on Amelia Island to prevent them from raising an alarm and alerting the British to their presence there.[24] Hoping to avert any advance of British troops from the south, Colonel Elbert ordered some men to reconnoiter the southern end of the island. Elbert's men were ambushed by a party of armed loyalists, resulting in one officer killed and two wounded.[25] Angered over the loss of his officer, Elbert burned every structure on Amelia Island and slaughtered all the livestock so that the British could not use them.[26] Amid the rebel attack, the island's slave population fled to St. Augustine.[27] Securing Amelia Island, Elbert was eager to press farther into East Florida. To his dismay, he discovered that he could not safely land his men on the southern banks of the St. Johns River without subjecting them to British cannon fire. Crown ships guarded the St. Johns River where British cannon fortified the southern banks, blocking any safe rebel naval operations there.[28] While Elbert's plans collapsed, a sea battle took place at the mouth of the St. Johns River between the British *Rebecca* and a sixteen-gun rebel brigantine.[29] The two ships exchanged cannon fire until the *Rebecca* successfully shot the rebels' topmast. Abandoning any hope of winning the struggle, the Americans decided to escape. British riflemen fired upon the rebels as they fled.[30] American dead littered the deck of their own ship. Two more rebels were spotted dead while falling from the tops of their ship into the sea.[31] Among the *Rebecca's* casualties, only one man died, and nine others wounded.[32]

When push came to shove, Elbert called off East Florida's invasion. His decision stemmed from a variety of reasons. The British were too well prepared, Georgia's frontier would be left defenseless, the Americans were low on supplies, and the heat made soldiering unbearable.[33] Instead of heading south to St. Augustine, Colonel Elbert took his men up the St. Marys River. He remained there for a few weeks, protecting Georgia's southern border from British raids, before finally abandoning that mission altogether.[34] In mid-July, his men crossed the Altamaha River, officially ending the second American invasion of East Florida. In the wake of the invasion, not one of Georgia's leaders took responsibility for the expedition's failure. Meanwhile, British leadership in Whitehall ordered Tonyn to attack Georgia. In August, the East Florida Rangers, accompanied by Seminole warriors, invaded Georgia's southern frontier. By that time, southern Georgia was so ravaged by war, loyalist raiders operated in that region without much difficulty. At one point, the Rangers were within five miles of Savannah, the state capital. The loyalist raiders were virtually unstoppable.[35] As British raids continued throughout the rest of the year, Georgia's residents were at the mercy of East Florida's raiders.

Separate from the military activity occurring in and around the Florida-Georgia border in 1777, the Minorcans of New Smyrna played out their respective role in the American Revolutionary War in East Florida. In 1777, some Minorcans joined Tonyn's East Florida Rangers—a result Tonyn so desired and personally lobbied for since the corps' formation in 1776. Well known to the locals of New Smyrna Beach, the region's settlement by European colonizers dates to 1768 when Scottish physician Andrew Turnbull led a colonization effort to Britain's far-flung outpost in North America. After a trip to Asia Minor and the Mediterranean, Turnbull married Maria Gracia Dura Bin from Greece. While in the Mediterranean, Turnbull hatched the idea of colonizing Florida with Mediterranean folk, people from a climate similar to that of Florida and skilled in the raising of semitropical products.[36] Turnbull immediately recruited colonists after securing financial backing for his vision and twenty thousand acres of land on the Florida frontier.[37] Most settlers who agreed to go with him were from the island of Minorca.[38] For many Minorcans, Turnbull offered an escape from the famine that swept their island.[39] In total, 1,403 people sailed under

Turnbull's patronage in the spring of 1768.[40] Turnbull spent £24,000 transporting all his colonists to East Florida.[41] After arriving at St. Augustine, Turnbull made the decision to settle Mosquito Inlet[42] (now known as the Ponce de Leon Inlet), establishing New Smyrna in early August.[43]

According to William Bartram, New Smyrna was established on a "high shelly bluff, on the West bank of the South branch of Musquito river."[44] During the time of Bartram's visit, the area was a large orange grove containing "oaks, magnolias, palms, [and] red bays."[45] Upon their arrival, the colonists were under contractual obligation to work for Turnbull for a number of years until they were granted their freedom; in the meantime, they were allowed to retain half of the crops they raised.[46] Life at the plantation was not what the colonists had

Portrait of Dr. Andrew Turnbull, New Smyrna, Florida, ca. 1870 (State Archives of Florida).

expected. New Smyrna had to literally be carved out of the wilderness. To give perspective on how deep into the frontier this settlement was, St. Augustine was seventy miles north of the colony. The need, then, to establish a working settlement was of the utmost importance. Until the cultivation of crops became a reality, the land would not support them. The work of carving out civilization in the Florida tropics demanded hard work. Turnbull employed overseers, former British army noncommissioned officers, to keep the settlers (his investment) working. Hard days were met with a scarcity of available food. Sure, there existed plenty of fish in the lagoons, but the settlers were not permitted to divert time and energy away from constructing a plantation, which they worked on seven days a week—often receiving no days for rest. Those poor colonists who dared lag behind optimal productivity endured harsh punishments including floggings.[47]

As they found out soon after their arrival, settlers suffered brutal working conditions, which contributed to a high death rate. Other factors that caused numerous deaths were starvation, scurvy, dropsy, unsanitary work conditions, yellow fever, typhoid fever, and pneumonia.[48] After a long day's work in the hot summer heat with the sun beating down on their necks, mosquitos visited the settlement at night, sometimes carrying malaria. Settlers wore rags and slept on bedding found to be in poor condition. For the first couple of years, New Smyrna settlers were forced to live in huts with sand floors, but by 1777 the colony boasted 145 houses. Conditions at the colony were so bad that the settlers, who felt imprisoned, led an unsuccessful revolt before their first year was over. By 1777, 964 deaths were

1953 photo of ruins of a warehouse at Turnbull's plantation (State Archives of Florida).

recorded at New Smyrna from the roughly 1,400 who came with Turnbull in 1768.[49] To make matters worse, New Smyrna colonists reported that Turnbull refused to honor their contracts after they expired, forcing them to work despite the end of their indentures.[50] In spite of their slave-like treatment, Minorcans were not an enslaved work force, nor were they servants. They were a temporary work force of free people—at least from a legal perspective.[51] Regardless of their status, life for Minorcans at New Smyrna was deprived, primitive, and characterized by constant struggle.

When Patrick Tonyn became governor of East Florida, he harbored reservations about East Florida's defensibility. As far as Tonyn was concerned, the colony was nearly indefensible.[52] To counter East Florida's weakness, Tonyn organized a militia battalion made up of loyalist refugees from the northern colonies.[53] "Attested to serve three Years or during the Rebellious

Troubles-" they would bolster East Florida's defenses.[54] Tonyn sought to raise four companies of men from among the people of African descent in the colony, plus two companies from the Saint Johns River, and four from St. Augustine.[55] Tonyn considered raising a company of Minorcans as well, but he was suspicious of their loyalties to the Crown. In a letter to Lord George Germain, Secretary of State for America in Lord North's Cabinet, Tonyn stated, "I am credibly informed, that they have invited the Rebels in Georgia, to come to their relief, and deliverance, and have promised their assistance."[56] Turnbull's nephew, then manager of New Smyrna while Dr. Turnbull was away, even expressed his concern in a private letter: "there is a good number of [New Smyrna colonists] at present a little discontented, and I am fully perswaded would Join the Rebels immediately on their landing at Smyrna."[57] Turnbull Jr. was so concerned he requested an additional eight to ten British regulars to bolster the garrison already stationed at New Smyrna.[58] Tonyn complained to Germain about sending additional soldiers to the settlement; after all, soldiers were much needed north to defend the Florida-Georgia border.[59] Colonel Robert Bisset, a British officer stationed in East Florida, attested to New Smyrna's indefensibility, which was largely due to the settlement's lack of arms and ammunition. According to Bisset, the situation in New Smyrna was "very alarming especially with regard to Dr. Turnbull's people, a great many of whom would certainly Join [the rebels]."[60] Bisset assured Tonyn that he would go to New Smyrna and arm trustworthy settlers and disarm suspected rebel sympathizers.[61]

Ambitious to tap into the manpower residing in New

Smyrna, Tonyn tempted the settlers to join his militia with offers of land, freedom, and protection if they abandoned their lot with Turnbull.[62] Of course, in letters to Germain, Tonyn played innocent against his true intentions of bolstering his militia ranks.[63] In March 1777, a few settlers escaped New Smyrna while Turnbull was away in England and arrived at St. Augustine seeking an audience with Governor Tonyn to confess their grievances of life at the settlement.[64] What followed was a months-long process of handling complaints issued by the settlers against Turnbull and his overseers. Some of the accusations were horrid and detail the sufferings endured by the colonists, which included "cruelties and murders." What followed was a rapid succession of events that ultimately contributed to New Smyrna's demise. The East Florida courts ruled in favor of Dr. Turnbull and ordered the settlers to return to their indentures.[65] In July 1777, Tonyn told Germain that the New Smyrna settlers were liberated on account of "conditional" and "shocking" circumstances. He informed the Secretary of State that small lots of land would be given to families of the freed settlers.[66] In reality, Tonyn disregarded the court's decision to return the indentured New Smyrna workers back to their master's plantation and instead encouraged the colonists to settle in St. Augustine where he assured them that he would protect them. As a result of Tonyn's murky treatment of the law, the Minorcans left New Smyrna for St. Augustine. During their time in the colony's capital, they were almost forgotten. Land was never doled out and many were forced to beg in the streets or find sustenance in fishing—they were wholly ignored by Tonyn.[67] Some managed to find work in East

Florida's provincial navy.[68] The section of the city where the Minorcans resided en masse became known as the "Minorcan Quarter" or the "Greek Quarter."[69] Desperate for coin, many joined the East Florida Rangers.[70] Some were dispatched to the Florida-Georgia border where they helped Indians scalp American settlers.[71] Turnbull was furious, charging Tonyn as the reason for his plantation's collapse.[72] In the end, Tonyn got what he wanted out of Turnbull's colonists: men for his loyalist militia.

Even after the Minorcan exodus, some settlers remained; New Smyrna was still in operation and produce continued to be exported from the plantation.[73] To this day, the city of New Smyrna Beach in Florida stands on the former settlement founded by Turnbull. He later left Florida after it was ceded to the Spanish and would go on to petition a compensation claim Parliament had offered to former British East Florida colonists who had lost land in the Spanish secession. He won £916. After East Florida's evacuation, Turnbull moved to Charleston, South Carolina, where he was permitted to remain as a British subject after the former colony officially became a state. He died on March 13, 1792, in Charleston.[74] As for the Minorcans, some fled with the loyalists and resettled in the Bahamas, Dominica, and Europe. Most of them, however, stayed behind, choosing to convert to the Catholic religion and become Spanish subjects.[75]

Taken together, the Minorcans lived out the drama that unfolded between East Florida's leaders during the American Revolutionary War. Put in a precarious situation and far from their native home, some Minorcans served the British during the war, but not out of true loyalty. Most served the Crown out of desperation and to avoid a bitter death in a harsh, war-torn, scarcely populated frontier colony that rested on the far-flung fringes of the British Empire. The reluctance of many Minorcans to evacuate with the British speaks volumes about not only their lack of commitment to the British, but also the loyalty they had for each other and their community. For many Minorcans, most of what they did, they did together. They endured the brutality of New Smyrna's overseers together, they petitioned Tonyn against their injustices suffered at Turnbull's plantation together, most abandoned New Smyrna together to live under Tonyn's protection, and many remained in Spanish Florida together after the British departure in the 1780s. The rest is history. Minorcan descendants still live in St. Augustine, Florida, to this day, where they continue to represent a large portion of the city's population.[76]

IV

The Battle of Alligator Creek Bridge and the Third American Invasion of East Florida, 1778

Since January 1778, Georgia leaders again talked of invading East Florida.[1] Congress officially approved an invasion in February, after which plans immediately went into effect to outfit an expedition.[2] In March 1778, Georgia's assembly confiscated the property of loyalist families who refused to sign oaths of allegiance. In Georgia, many women and children lived on homesteads while their husbands or fathers fought for the British on the Florida-Georgia border. On March 9, Georgia leaders offered commissions to any individual willing to lead forays into East Florida. That same day, Georgia's assembly attempted to induce occupation of the St. Marys River by offering interested settlers five-hundred-acre land grants. This policy was unpopular. No one took the offer. This inducement points to the alleged influence the Georgia assembly thought it had in the region. Control of the St. Marys River, after all, certainly did not belong to the rebels.[3]

In March 1778, Brown's East Florida Rangers and their Indian allies patrolled the area in and around the St. Marys River. Operating out of Fort Tonyn, the Rangers and bands of Native warriors raided Georgian plantations, stealing horses and cattle.

On either March 12 or March 13, Thomas Brown, one hundred of his men, and ten Indian warriors attacked Fort Howe, deep in rebel territory.[4] Brown and his force swam across the Altamaha River, clutching their powder high above their heads to ensure that none of it got wet. The Rangers reconnoitered the fort at night. The following morning, either on March 13 or March 14, Brown and his men attacked Fort Howe. During the battle, one Ranger was killed and four were wounded. The British managed to kill two Americans, wound four, and capture twenty-three. Unfortunately for Brown, he did not have sufficient manpower to occupy and maintain a provisioned garrison at the fort. Consequently, he burned it and destroyed the artillery, rendering both useless.[5] The loss of Fort Howe reduced all Georgian forts south of the Altamaha River. Its loss also allowed Brown and his Rangers unmolested access to South Carolina loyalists.[6] After the battle, Brown proceeded north to reestablish communications with loyalist garrisons in South Carolina.[7] Through his intelligence gathering, Brown discovered six thousand loyalist inhabitants in the Carolinas who were ready to fight.[8] Pointing to their significance, these large concentrations of loyalist forces in the southern colonies prompted London officials to adopt a southern strategy during the second half of the American Revolution.[9] Brown returned to St. Augustine, bringing back valuable information on Carolina loyalists and Georgia's military strength. Brown's operations gave loyalists virtually unmolested access to freely travel through Georgia. During the entirety of 1778, seven thousand loyalists made their way to East Florida from the Carolinas.[10]

In April, Washington approved a third invasion of East

Florida.[11] Washington's decision came at a critical juncture. Indeed, the alarming situation on Georgia's frontier demanded a response. Consequently, the third American invasion force, commanded by Brigadier-General Robert Howe, mobilized in no time. Colonel Samuel Elbert, a veteran of the previous year's invasion of East Florida, was placed under Howe's command. A Georgia militia of 1,200 under Georgia governor John Houstoun supplemented the Continental regulars. In total, Howe and Houstoun raised roughly three thousand men.[12] By April 9, American forces camped among Fort Howe's charred remains. While rebel troops marched overland, another force advanced by sea. A small flotilla, comprised of the *Washington*, the *Lee*, and the *Bulloch*, sailed down Georgia's coast and attacked Frederica on St. Simons Island. On the morning of April 19, the Americans descended on three British ships anchored off Frederica's coast.[13] Caught off guard, the British surrendered. Two important vessels were captured in this attack, the *Hinchinbrook* and the *Rebecca*. As a result of this important action, East Florida, at the time, was left with only three vessels, the *Galatea*, the *Perseus*, and the *Daphne*.[14]

As the American threat drew nearer, feuds between East Florida's leadership produced a less-than-desirable defensive reality. On April 21, General Prevost stationed British regulars along the St. Johns River, refusing to place them at the St. Marys alongside Brown's Rangers.[15] Prevost's conflict with Tonyn over control of the East Florida Rangers points to his refusal to cooperate with the governor.[16] Prevost disliked the fact that Thomas Brown outranked several officers under his command. In eighteenth-

Portrait of British General Augustine Prevost, ca. 1770 (State Archives of Florida).

century British North America, provincial and regular officers of the same rank were subordinate to the regular officers. However, lower-ranking British officers were subordinate to higher-ranking provincial officers. British officers commonly believed they should not be ordered by provincial officers of higher rank. For that reason, no British regulars were stationed on the St. Marys River in April, which would have constituted Britain's first line of defense against the Americans. As far as the navy was concerned, Tonyn purchased three ships in 1778, the *Germaine*, the *Dreadnaught*, and the *Thunderer*, to augment East Florida's "critical situation regarding the lack of coastal and riverine defense."[17] The crews agreed to split whatever profits they managed to secure on duty.[18]

With the Americans moving south, Thomas Brown ordered Captain James Moore and a party of Indians and seventy-six Rangers to circle around the rebels and attack them from the rear. While operating behind enemy lines, Moore was betrayed by one of his own. The rebels captured the captain and murdered him.[19] His men managed to escape. Back at the rebel camp, thirty South Carolina loyalists seeking asylum in East Florida joined the American invasion force. Under the protection of the American army, they traveled south across the no man's land between Georgia and Florida. No bandits, they reasoned, would dare attack an army. Upon reaching East Florida, the loyalists' plan was to desert the rebels and flee to the safety of St. Augustine. According to Siebert, one of their rank snuck away to scout out a path. He never returned. The remaining loyalists abandoned their escape plan, choosing to stay with the Americans instead.[20]

While Howe consolidated his forces at Fort Howe, desertions occurred daily. Apprehended mutineers and those inciting and encouraging mutiny were shot or hung. On June 1, Howe and his men celebrated France's public acknowledgment of America's independence with thirteen cannon blasts and alcohol. By mid-June a majority of the rebel invasion force still resided in Georgia. On June 17, Brown's East Florida Rangers engaged a rebel scouting party at the St. Johns River.[21] Further east, on June 24, an American force landed at Fernandina on Amelia Island. Unable to stop the American advance, the British retired to the St. Johns Bluff, intending to halt the rebels there.[22] British lieutenant colonel Fuser, the officer charged with defending Amelia Island, blamed the island's loss on East Florida's loyalist inhabitants who refused to join the militia. According to Fuser, when he called on loyalist support, specifically among those who had not yet enlisted in the militia, none offered their help.[23]

On June 28, the Americans reached the St. Marys River. They remained there for a few hours while Howe and Houstoun argued over where to march next. On June 29, they arrived at Fort Tonyn.[24] Finding the fort abandoned, they camped there overnight. In nearby Cabbage Swamp, Brown and his Rangers hid out, subsisting on palmetto roots.[25] Brown refused to give the rebels an inch of East Florida ground. He ordered his men to harass the Americans as much as possible.[26] The nearest British military detail was about fourteen miles away at Alligator Creek Bridge.[27] Aware that Brown was unable to survive indefinitely in Cabbage Swamp, two hundred British regulars were dispatched from Alligator Creek Bridge to rescue Brown and his men.[28] On June 30, the East Florida Rangers withdrew from Cabbage Swamp to rendezvous with British forces at Alligator Creek Bridge.[29]

Major Mark Prevost guarded Alligator Creek Bridge with a force of 450 regulars from the 16th and 60th Regiments, Grenadiers from the Second Battalion, and various South Carolina Royalists.[30] A trench encircled the British camp there. Entanglements of logs and brush added an extra layer of protection.[31] On June 30, around noon, British soldiers cleaned their guns and bathed in the creek while the Grenadiers worked on a breastwork. A bridge connected the king's road across Alligator Creek. As Brown's Rangers crossed the bridge, those at the rear started running for the British line. Behind them, three hundred rebel cavalry under the command of General James Screven were in hot pursuit.[32] For a moment, British sentries standing guard at Alligator Bridge thought the advancing rebel cavalry were allies. Since the East Florida Rangers wore no uniforms, the sentries mistakenly assumed the rebel cavalry were just more of Brown's men.[33] Once they realized their mistake, British troops sprang into action. According to a British soldier at the scene, the rebel cavalrymen flourished their weapons and shouted, "Down with the Tories!"[34] Brown's Rangers jumped behind the redoubt and opened fire on the oncoming Americans. Other Rangers scattered in the swamps, intending to flank the rebels from the side. As the Rangers engaged the American cavalry, British drummers played "British Grenadiers," while the regulars fetched their muskets. Replacing the Rangers on the breastworks, British regulars opened fire on the rebels. This freed up Brown and the rest of his men to enter the swamps and flank the enemy. After noticing that he and his men were about to be surrounded, General Screven ordered a retreat. Major Prevost ordered his men not to pursue.[35] At the end of the battle, the British killed three Americans, captured one, and wounded nine others. British losses amounted to only one dead and eight wounded.[36]

Burton Barrs believes that if the Americans pressed their attack, they would have achieved victory. This assertion is dubious, especially considering that the British fought behind cover and outnumbered the rebels by at least 150 men, and that is not counting Brown's Rangers or any of their Indian allies. The next day, Major Prevost abandoned his position on

Alligator Creek Bridge and withdrew south with his men to Trout Creek. According to Barrs, Major Prevost's position at Trout Creek was roughly six miles northeast of Cowford on the St. Johns River.[37] As they went, the British felled trees to cover the road and hinder any efficient southward rebel movement or pursuit.[38] Indians were left behind to observe and maintain intelligence of the area.[39]

Back at the American camp, sickness—notably malaria and dysentery—plagued the rebel soldiers. Provisions were in short supply and disorganization haunted progress. The militia and Continental soldiers suffered a strained relationship. Militia units regularly disobeyed orders from Continental officers. As the Americans encamped on the St. Marys River, rebel leadership disagreed on what to do next. General Howe and the other Continental officers wanted to withdraw, Governor John Houstoun wanted to attack St. Augustine directly, and Colonel Andrew Williamson, a militia officer, would go no further than the St. Johns River. At length, Howe and the other Continental officers decided among themselves to abandon the invasion. They reasoned that because of general sickness, the inability of rebel naval operations occurring past the Amelia Narrows, the lack of expedition leader concurrance on important points, and the fact that the British had been pushed out of Georgia, no military operation against East Florida could afford to continue. On July 14, General Howe marched his Continental soldiers away from East Florida. The sick and wounded were put on boats and ferried north. Without the Continental army's support, the Georgia militia did not have sufficient strength to continue. They, too, packed up and withdrew.[40] In consequence, the third and final rebel invasion of East Florida ended in failure. In total, half of the men who accompanied the expedition became ill and five hundred were lost, three hundred of which were South Carolinians.[41]

In the wake of the failed American attempt to conquer East Florida, Tonyn took the fight to Georgia. General Augustine Prevost advised caution and refused to cooperate in military operations with Tonyn north of the St. Johns River. Prevost was not against invasion per se, but he preferred to wait for direct orders from his superiors and the arrival of reinforcements before he would agree to do anything.[42] Proceeding ahead without Prevost, Tonyn sent Brown's Rangers on raiding missions into Georgia.[43] Indian war parties stalked the East Florida–Georgia frontier. Five hundred Seminole warriors patrolled north of the St. Johns River while parties of Upper and Lower Creeks went on the offensive. Some war parties got as far north as Sunbury.[44] These warriors were not loose bands of Natives who struck isolated settlements. No. They were large war parties capable of taking on garrisoned forts. One war party managed to sack and burn a Georgian outpost on the Satilla River.[45] On August 30, back in East Florida, a rogue privateer seized thirty African American slaves from New Smyrna.[46] Two ships, the *Otter* and the *George*, set out after them. Both ships were lost in a violent storm off the coast of Cape Canaveral.[47] While the ships did not survive, the crew did.[48] Rebel privateers continued threatening East Florida during the war. In one instance, a privateer crashed north of New Smyrna. The fifty survivors were captured and imprisoned in St. Augustine.[49]

On August 31, the Georgian government relocated all loyalist families to fortified plantations scattered around the state. The loyalist women and children who remained in huts within Georgia while their husbands and fathers were away at war were suspected of ferrying information across the border to the British in East Florida.[50] Reports describing Britain's southern strategy alarmed rebel officials. According to British leaders in Parliament, staunch support for the Crown existed in the southern colonies. Whitehall decided to incorporate southern loyalists into their plans for bringing the southern colonies back under British control. London would commence its southern strategy by recapturing Savannah, Georgia. British troops from New York would be channeled away from the northern colonies and sent to Savannah.[51] Loyalists and Indians in East Florida would invade Georgia from the south, while a separate Indian army attacked Augusta from the western frontier and rendezvoused with British troops in Savannah.[52] Once Savannah was recaptured, an amalgamate force of British regulars, loyalists, and Indians would move north and take Charleston. Savannah and Charleston could then be used as bases to launch invasions of North Carolina and Virginia. The southern strategy relied on loyalists holding and garrisoning captured territory.[53] Crown officials believed thousands of loyalists would flock to the British standard and pledge their support. In cooperation with British troops, Whitehall reckoned, loyalists would regain control of the southern colonies and restore their own civil government.[54]

While the British planned their southern strategy, the Continental Congress proposed a fourth invasion of East Florida in the summer of 1778, the second such invasion that year.[55] The Continental Congress was motivated by Indian and loyalist raids, the loss of property, and intelligence reports that indicated the British were planning a counter-invasion of the southern colonies.[56] Congress approved the invasion in November.[57] General Jean-Baptiste Donatien, Comte de Rochambeau, urged Washington to abandon the prospect of invading East Florida. He believed that there was not enough time to put together an effective expedition in such short notice.[58] Convinced, Washington abandoned the mission.

In preparation for the upcoming southern campaign, Tonyn expected British troops to land in St. Augustine. As it stood, St. Augustine did not have enough supplies to care for a surge in the city's population. Like before, British East Florida leaders looked north to remedy their delicate food situation. On November 19, General Prevost dispatched his brother Major Mark Prevost to Georgia with one hundred regulars, three hundred East Florida Rangers, and various Indians. Major Prevost was ordered deep into rebel territory to collect livestock north of the Altamaha River around the Midway and Newport settlements. In light of recent forays into Georgia over the last few years, the southern frontier was devoid of any livestock, making such a dangerous mission necessary. While Major Prevost advanced north, Lieutenant Colonel Lewis Fuser commanded a diversionary force instructed to move against the town of Sunbury. On November 24, Prevost engaged an American force as he approached Midway. A party of East Florida Rangers ambushed, wounded, and captured rebel general James Screven. Screven died from his wounds the next day.[59] Some reports of the incident claim that angry Rangers descended upon Screven and shot him some more, discharging their weapons at point-blank range while he lay on the ground.[60] The British position in the region now compromised, Major Prevost was concerned about a prolonged engagement at Midway Church. Deep in rebel territory, Whig reinforcements could arrive and overwhelm the British at any moment. With a stroke of luck, the outnumbered rebel force withdrew. Advancing unopposed, the British found Midway Church abandoned. Eager to leave, Prevost ordered a retreat. Before departing, Prevost burned the Midway Meeting House, a symbolic gesture as well as a practical one, since the rebels stored their munitions there. On their way south, Prevost rustled about two thousand livestock and captured two hundred African American slaves. At length, Major Prevost's invasion was a success. Lieutenant Colonel Fuser's diversionary tactics produced few measurable results. By the time Fuser caught wind of Prevost's retreat, his force of five hundred men, accompanied by artillery, occupied the town of Sunbury proper.[61] All of Sunbury's inhabitants remained behind the safety of their fort's walls. When Fuser demanded their surrender, the defenders replied, "come and take it."[62] Fuser declined to assault the fort. Instead, he turned around and marched back to East Florida.[63]

On November 27, 1778, a large British force under Lieutenant Colonel Archibald Campbell set sail from New York, bound for Georgia's conquest.[64] The British meant to launch an amphibious assault against Savannah while East Florida's forces invaded Georgia from the south. Immediately after his return to East Florida, Major Prevost was given command of nine hundred men and ordered once more into Georgia. This time, his objectives were two-fold: level the port town of Sunbury and rendezvous with Campbell's forces in Savannah.[65] Prevost marched into Georgia unopposed. The army's supplies were ferried on boats along the coast. These boats were sometimes forced to go around armed rebel vessels. Consequently, they were not always able to provide the Florida troops with their necessary provisions. When supplies were not available, Prevost's men subsisted on oysters and rice.[66] In time, the British found themselves before Sunbury. The British laid siege to the fort at Sunbury on January 7, 1779. On the third day of the siege, the fort's garrison sallied out, but they were driven back. The British bombarded the fort with cannon fire until the rebels surrendered on January 10. The British reported one dead and three wounded while rebel losses amounted to three dead, six wounded, and 212 captured.[67] Additionally, British troops rounded up a hundred prisoners near the vicinity of the fort.[68] Four rebel naval vessels were also captured.[69] Once Major Prevost secured Sunbury, he and his men moved on to Savannah to join Lieutenant Colonel Campbell, who had taken control of the city on December 29, 1778.[70] Major Prevost arrived there on January 17, 1779.[71] Prevost and his men were referred to as the "Florida Brigade."[72] Lieutenant Colonel Archibald Campbell disparagingly called the Florida troops "rag tag and Bobtails."[73] In addition to Major Prevost's land forces, Tonyn also sent some of East Florida's navy, including the *Germain*, *Spitfire*, *Delight*, *Thunderer*, and a few other unnamed vessels, to assist in Savannah's recapture.[74]

Shortly after his arrival to Savannah, Major Prevost was appointed lieutenant governor of Georgia. He would also serve as acting governor of Georgia during Governor James Wright's absence.[75] The East Florida Rangers were reorganized and renamed the King's Carolina Rangers.[76] They would continue to fight the rebels in the southern colonies along with Thomas Brown, who would later shatter his arm and suffer wounds on both his thighs. Brown would be appointed superintendent of the southern Indian department after John Stuart's death on March 21, 1779.[77] After Stuart's demise, the office of the superintendent for the southern Indian department was split in two, recognizing a western and eastern superintendent. Brown was appointed the eastern superintendency.[78]

The conclusion of 1778 produced a dramatic turn of events for British fortune in East Florida. After the third and final American invasion of East Florida ended in failure, the rebels never again attempted to invade that province. After the British recaptured Savannah in December 1778, Georgia and the Carolinas absorbed the American Revolutionary conflict that otherwise would have probably continued in and around East Florida. The presence of British troops in Savannah and later Charleston would prove too much of an immediate threat to the rebels, dispelling the materialization of any serious invasion of out-of-the-way East Florida.

V

British East Florida's Final Years, 1779–1785

The return to Georgia's pre-revolutionary normalcy under British control diminished East Florida's presence in the American Revolution. However, the province was not completely forgotten. In May 1779, Benjamin Franklin and the Marquis de Lafayette compiled a list outlining various cruelties the British inflicted on Americans. Governor Tonyn's payment for Georgian scalps is among those cruelties listed.[1] By 1780, George Washington once more sought East Florida's conquest.[2] On January 28–29, 1780, Major General Benjamin Lincoln, then stationed in Charleston, wrote to Washington, advising the commander-in-chief against an invasion of East Florida. Major General Lincoln believed "it would be embarrassing, and unsafe to attempt an expedition against that Province."[3] Ultimately, the 1780 plans to invade East Florida collapsed in large part because of the threat General Charles Cornwallis posed as he and his army advanced north through the Carolinas.[4]

After the British recaptured Savannah in 1778, some loyalists migrated back to Georgia.[5] Former residents, displaced by wartime raids, returned to the St. Marys River.[6] The loyalist repopulation of Georgia emboldened Tonyn to consider annexing all the land between the St. Marys and Altamaha Rivers to East Florida. These aspirations never materialized. With British troops in Savannah, East Floridians no longer feared an American invasion from the north. Georgia now served as a buffer colony between East Florida and rebel forces in the Carolinas.

A threat to East Florida did exist, however, to the west. On June 21, 1779, Spain declared war on Great Britain. Prior to 1779, London officials tried to keep Spain out of the fight. Britain attempted to buy Spain's neutrality by hinting at possibly handing over Gibraltar or the Floridas. At one point, Britain even threatened to destabilize South America by inciting rebellions throughout the continent. All these efforts ultimately failed. Despite her coming into the war, Spain did not enter into a formal alliance with the United States. According to J. Leitch Wright Jr., while Spain supported the United States throughout the war, she never officially treated the United States like an independent nation.[7] After Spain entered the war, Britain was forced to contend with one more European power.

From New Orleans, Spaniards marched on West Florida. A large force under Bernardo de Galvez, the Spanish governor of New Orleans, intended to conquer West Florida for Spain. In 1781, West Florida fell to Galvez, and from that point forward Spanish West Florida threatened East Florida's status as a British colony. Rumors of Spanish invasion plans for East Florida circled around St. Augustine in 1780 and 1781.[8] Alarmed at the prospect of losing East Florida to the Spanish, Lieutenant Colonel Alured Clarke, then stationed in Savannah, dispatched a force of Hessian soldiers from the Garrison Regiment von Knoblauch to St. Augustine.[9] Despite Spain's presence in the west, East Florida remained British for the remainder of the war. Unknown to Tonyn at the time, Spain was preoccupied with West Florida, the Bahamas, and Jamaica.[10] What's more, domestic rebellions in South America hindered Spain's effectiveness in the Revolutionary War, destroying any real efforts Spain otherwise could have had in capturing East Florida.[11] Make no mistake, Spain wanted East Florida and even planned her acquisition. Tonyn's fears were well founded. In fact, in 1779, Spanish officials pushed the United States Congress to attack East Florida.[12]

Spanish motivation to invade East Florida no doubt came from their intelligence gathering in that province. Spanish spies in East Florida usually came from Havana.[13] Spies in St. Augustine regularly delivered reports to Spanish officials in Havana. Cuban fishermen transferred these reports under the guise of delivering holy oil for the Minorcan Catholics.[14] One of those spies, Luciano de Herrera, lived in St. Augustine during the First Spanish Period. He remained in St. Augustine after Florida became British.[15] Tonyn eventually discovered Herrera's deception, but before he could do anything, Herrera fled to Havana.[16] Juan Jose Eligio de la Puente, a Spanish botanist and adventurer, was also a spy in the Revolutionary War. Puente visited East Florida many times between 1776 and 1778 to "investigate" Florida's flora and fauna. On these trips, Puente gathered information on East Florida's military strength. He produced various plans for assaulting St. Augustine and made maps to go along with his reports.

In the spring of 1780, East Florida was afflicted with smallpox.[17] Residents were quickly inoculated. An unreported number died, but the mortality rate was "scarcely felt."[18]

In 1779, Tonyn advocated for the formation of East Florida's general assembly.[19] Between a failed joint American-French attack on Savannah in October 1779, the explosion of East Florida's population from loyalist refugees, and the fact that dissension within East Florida's government from William Drayton and Andrew Turnbull subsided, Tonyn finally decided East Florida was politically safe enough to form a general assembly.[20] Despite Tonyn's advocation for the formation of a lower house, the prospect languished in limbo until February 1781. Shortly thereafter, a province-wide summons ordered all male inhabitants over the age of twenty-one and who owned at least fifty acres of land report to the St. Augustine courthouse between four and six o'clock from March 13 to 16, 1781, to vote on the members of East Florida's general assembly. After the elections, the first East Florida general assembly met at St. Augustine on

Monument erected in Saint Augustine to Minorcan Catholics (State Archives of Florida).

March 27, 1781, and lasted until November 12, 1781. For Tonyn, the general assembly proved to be more trouble than it was worth. Legislative disagreements broke down any cooperation between the upper and lower houses.[21] Particularities over the regulation of African slaves caused the political rift in the assembly.[22] Essentially, the lower house wanted to try slaves charged with capital crimes in local district courts. The upper house refused and thus a quarrel ensued. Tension became so heated, the lower house threatened to suspend issuing revenue to the province and to cease all tax collection until the upper house conceded to their wishes. Infuriated, the upper house charged the lower house with acting unparliamentary and exercising unjust coercion. In the wake of bad times in provincial government, Tonyn dissolved East Florida's assembly.[23]

The assembly briefly reconvened in October 1781. Tonyn dissolved the assembly again on November 12, 1781, when the upper and lower houses refused to cooperate.[24] London officials were not pleased when the Board of Trade caught wind of Tonyn's dissolution of the assembly. The board believed that dissolving the assembly accomplished nothing. A second general assembly met in January 1782 and lasted until its last meeting on March 25, 1784. During its brief existence, East Florida's assembly passed some important legislation. Laws were issued concerning militia regulation, ordering all males between the ages of fifteen and sixty to serve. Slaves from local plantations were directed to work on St. Augustine's fortifications, various municipal codes were created, and revenue acts were enforced.[25] A bill that reverted uncultivated lands back to the Crown was also introduced, which would have stimulated

East Florida's settlement, growth, and development. While this bill never saw the light of day, it would have fixed East Florida's absentee planter problem. During the general assembly's last meeting, Tonyn addressed the assemblymen and concluded, "I shall forever retain the greatest attachment for and regard to his Majesty's ever faithful subjects, the loyal people of East-Florida."[26]

King George III considered Cornwallis's surrender at Yorktown only a temporary setback. The king wanted to continue warring with the rebelling North American colonies, much in contrary to the prevailing opinions in Parliament against a prolonged war.[27] By 1782, London realized she would not be able to subdue her North American rebellion. Consequently, peace talks between Britain, Spain, France, and the United States forever changed the history of East Florida. In December 1782, Tonyn and Indian Superintendent Thomas Brown held the last Indian war council within East Florida's borders. The council talked of peace and many presents were doled out.[28] The Treaty of Paris ended the American War of Independence on September 3, 1783. Article 5 ceded East Florida to Spain. East Florida was deemed worthless to most British Parliamentarians.[29] Lord Shelbourne believed that resisting Florida's loss was not worth the risk of "losing the peace."[30] After the treaty's ratification, Britain was given eighteen months to evacuate East Florida, settle accounts, and sell loyalist property. By 1783, East Florida's evacuation was underway. Between 1783 and 1785, East Florida's evacuation was disorganized and chaotic. The province's population, which surged as refugees from the southern colonies fled to St. Augustine, boasted 17,375 people in 1783.[31] Many loyalists from Georgia and the Carolinas who served the British in militia or provincial units brought their families to East Florida to escape the wrath of their neighbors after the British withdrew from the region. East Florida's evacuation was thus postponed, allowing these loyalists ample time to travel to St. Augustine and evacuate there. As early as May 1782, British commander-in-chief Sir Guy Carleton wanted to evacuate East Florida. Tonyn urged the need for East Florida to remain open so that the colony could absorb refugees. Carleton conceded and delayed East Florida's evacuation.[32]

On April 21 and April 29, 1783, Tonyn issued two separate proclamations informing East Florida's inhabitants of the colony's cession to Spain, the need for residents to evacuate and settle their debts, and that his majesty's vessels would evacuate loyalists to other colonies within the British Empire.[33] Definite evacuation orders, dated December 4, 1783, reached Tonyn in the spring of 1784. Tonyn published another proclamation on May 6, 1784, directing East Florida's inhabitants to apply for evacuation by May 29 to Lieutenant Colonel William Brown, commissioner of embarkation at St. Augustine, or to Lieutenant Robert Leaver, agent for transports at St. Marys, and receive embarkation instructions on the transport ships assigned to them.[34] Evacuation transports were provided at the public expense.[35] East Florida's inhabitants did not receive news of their resettlement well.[36] According to one St. Augustine resident, peace with the United States was "the severest shock our feelings have ever had to struggle with."[37] Many residents felt deserted and banished by their king, left without hope and cast off. One letter, written by M. Tattnall to John Street, dated

May 30, 1783, offers insight into the general feelings of East Florida's residents toward their orders to vacate the province. In his emotionally charged letter, Tattnall believed, Parliament abandoned her East Florida residents. He writes, "I shall ever, though, remember with satisfaction that it was not I deserted my King but my King that deserted me."[38]

For those Tories who worked hard to build a new life in East Florida, their efforts were in vain. "Heavens!" wrote one resident, "what distress . . . O Englishmen, where is now your national honour? Nothing but bribery, corruption and treason prevails in your senate who promised protection."[39] A breakdown in law and order followed the news of Spain's cession of East Florida. Rioting exploded across the province. In an attempt to quell rioters, East Florida's general assembly passed a law on January 25, 1783, forbidding anyone from selling beer, cider, brandy, rum, punch, or other strong liquors whatsoever "in less quantities than two gallons at one time."[40] Rumors that Florida would be traded for Gibraltar circled among residents.[41] Robbers and plunderers roamed the province in search of victims; angry soldiers threatened to mutiny, loot St. Augustine, and murder anyone who stood in their way—some soldiers were even killed in an attempt to execute this plan; angry Indians roamed St. Augustine's streets, unhappy with Spain's return; and bands of thieves and gangsters raided frontier plantations in the north end of the province.[42] Tonyn called these thugs "banditti," who were nothing more than "murderers and assassins."[43] Most of the bandits who raided East Florida's settlements were vagrants who robbed both Georgian and East Floridian plantations during the Revolutionary War. The most infamous gang was the McGirtt gang led by Daniel McGirtt, a former Georgian.[44] To restore order, Tonyn raised two Troops of Horse to check the gangs and roving marauders.[45] This militia engaged the bandits in many skirmishes and battles.[46] Some of McGirtt's gangsters were captured, but many escaped and hid in swamps.[47] The McGirtt gang was eventually apprehended by Spanish authorities, rounded up, and sent to Havana.[48]

Apart from armed raiders, a group of conspirators, led by John Cruden, talked on the St. Johns River of opposing East Florida's transfer to Spain. Cruden planned on overpowering Spanish officials once the transfer was complete. Cruden intended to send loyalist refugees into the southern colonies to recruit men for a small army. Meetings were held at St. Johns Town and on the St. Marys River. These meetings helped Cruden ascertain how many men he had at his disposal. Unfortunately for Cruden, he encountered many who wanted to take over whatever was left of East Florida's British government. Plans were hatched to overpower the British force at St. Augustine, capture Tonyn and other British officials, and then forcefully prevent any Spanish attempt to take control of East Florida. To prove their seriousness, the conspirators attacked two detachments of British troops stationed at an outpost on the St. Johns River. Conspirators killed one captain and one soldier from the first detachment while capturing sixteen men from the second detachment. This was too much for Cruden. He did not condone violence against the British king's troops. After these attacks, Cruden personally went to Tonyn himself and confessed everything he knew about the conspiracy. Tonyn, in response, placed Cruden in charge of rounding up and punishing the bandits. Not long after, the conspiracy was quickly shut down. Cruden, however, did not abandon his attempt at blocking Spain's cession of East Florida. In October 1784, Cruden petitioned Carlos III, or Charles III, the king of Spain, to allow the existence of an autonomous state between the St. Johns River and the St. Marys River.[49] It would be called "United Loyalist."[50] Carlos III did not pursue this idea.[51] Failing there, Cruden even applied to the state of Georgia, who considered Cruden's plans but never approved them.[52]

While East Florida descended into chaos, the Native Americans posed a serious threat to the British, so much so that Tonyn wanted to ensure they were appeased before he left. When West Florida fell to the Spanish, Great Britain's Indian allies were forced to travel all the way to St. Augustine, which became the new center of Indian diplomacy, gift-giving, and point of contact in the south. By 1783, thousands of Natives swarmed East Florida. During the British evacuation, roughly 3,000 Creeks, 1,200 Cherokees, 1,000 Choctaws and Chickasaws, and other delegations from the Seminole, Tuscarora, Mingo, Seneca, and Mohawk tribes all resided in St. Augustine. Unfortunately for these groups, Indians were not included in Revolutionary War peace talks. During the war, British agents promised the southern tribes protection for their lands and continued trade goods in exchange for their cooperation and friendship.[53] Britain's departure from East Florida meant that British agents could no longer deliver on past promises. In consequence, an Indian war loomed ominously over British East Florida. Given East Florida's chaotic and disorganized condition in its final years under British control, it is highly possible a large-scale, well-coordinated Indian attack could have erased the British presence from that province entirely. Some Indians requested to evacuate with the British.[54] After East Florida was turned over to Spain, an old Cherokee warrior told Governor Tonyn that if "the great man over the water [King George III] would give them large canoes and land for hunting," most of his nation would leave East Florida with the British.[55] Lower Creek chief Okaiegige angrily claimed that the British king sought to throw away East Florida. The chief reminded British officials that his people fought and lost many lives for the English and in return they were promised never to be forsaken. "Is the Great King conquered?" Okaiegige asked, "Or does he mean to abandon us? Or does he intend to treat his Friends as slaves, or only give our lands to his and our Enemies[?]" Cherokee chief Raven pointed out that "we have heard . . . that the English have given up our lands . . . to be divided amongst our Enemies. The Peacemakers and our Enemies have talked away our land at a Rum drinking."[56] This was mostly discouraged, but a small number of Native Americans managed to relocate in the Bahamas. One Cherokee mestizo chief lived in Thomas Brown's home in the Bahamas for a period of time.[57] To combat the chaos of evacuation, 150 British regulars from the 37th Regiment were dispatched from New York City and sent to St. Augustine to maintain the peace.[58] They arrived in East Florida on November 1, 1783.[59]

As East Florida's evacuation proceeded in earnest in 1784, British property holders had a hard time ridding themselves of their property. Most property sold at a loss. Indeed, the Spaniards were only interested in St. Augustine homes, and even those were selling at a quarter of their value. British residents who did not wish to abandon or give away their property left it in the hands of agents to sell at a more reasonable rate and send the proceeds later on.[60] Slave property was given its own consideration too. Official commissioners from Georgia and South Carolina came to East Florida from 1782 onward to recover slaves that had either run away or were kidnapped during the war.[61] Ultimately, only a few slaves were returned to their former masters.[62] Disputes over slave ownership were often chaotic.

Despite the danger, disorder, and disappointment that characterized British East Florida's evacuation, not everything in Britain's final years in that province was bad. In 1783, British East Florida's only newspaper was established. Titled the *East Florida Gazette*, it was sometimes referred to as the *East Florida Gazette Extraordinary*.[63] Only three editions of this paper exist today.[64] The paper was printed weekly from February 1, 1783, to March 22, 1784.[65] Before the *East Florida Gazette's* arrival, newspapers reached East Florida residents by ship. East Floridians primarily read the *Georgia Gazette* and/or the *Royal Georgia Gazette*.[66] William Wells, the founder and editor of the *East Florida Gazette*, resettled in the Bahamas after the war, where he established the *Bahama Gazette*.[67] Apart from a newspaper, East Florida also hosted four theatrical performances in 1783.[68] On March 3, 1783, the *East Florida Gazette* advertised two plays: *The Beaux' Stratagem* and *Miss in Her Teens*.[69] On May 20, 1783, the *East Florida Gazette* mentioned two more plays: *Douglas, a Tragedy* and the *Entertainment of Barnaby Brittle*.[70] The plays were put on "for the benefit of the distressed refugees."[71] The plays were scheduled to perform in the Government House. According to David Mays, *The Beaux' Stratagem* was most likely held in the assembly room where a temporary stage was constructed. The plays' directors most likely employed the bare minimum of scenery and props.[72] Performances began at 7:00 p.m. All roles were played by men.

Vol. I. THE

East-Florida GAZETTE.

Nullius Addictus Jurare In Verba Magistri. Hor.

From SATURDAY, April 26, to SATURDAY, May 3, 1783.

St. AUGUSTINE, May 3.

Front page of a May 1783 edition of the East Florida Gazette *(State Archives of Florida).*

In fact, many British officers starred in the shows because actresses were hard to come by.[73]

In addition to East Florida's rare cultural expression, Colonel Andrew Deveaux's Bahamas expedition stirred up some excitement. In 1782, Spanish forces captured the British Bahamas. Colonel Deveaux sought to invade the Bahamas in 1783 to recapture what was previously lost.[74] Historian Charles Mowat considers the 1783 invasion nothing but "theatrics," pointing out that the Bahamas were brought back under British control after peace was reached between Spain and Britain.[75] Indeed, Article V of the peace preliminaries at Versailles, agreed upon on January 20, 1783, by England, France, and Spain, turned the Bahamas back over to the British, rendering Deveaux's invasion unnecessary.[76] Deveaux was certainly not aware of the transfer because in March 1783 he set out for the Bahamas. In Deveaux's defense, news of the peace process had not yet reached St. Augustine by the time he set out with his army.[77]

Colonel Andrew Deveaux was a native-born American from Beaufort, South Carolina. He was the son of a wealthy planter. During the American Revolutionary War, Deveaux joined the British and, in their service, performed guerrilla warfare in the southern theater of the war.[78] In 1782, Deveaux and his men fled to the safety of St. Augustine after the British evacuation of Charleston and Savannah. He would not remain in St. Augustine long. In February 1783 Deveaux began gathering men, arms, uniforms, and provisions for his expedition to the Bahamas.[79] Deveaux paid for the expedition through his wealth accrued in South Carolina.[80] On March 30 Deveaux set sail from St. Augustine with roughly forty to seventy men, some of whom were Cherokee, Choctaw, and Seminole.[81] Six small vessels, captained by privateers, carried them from St. Augustine to New Providence.[82] The expedition recruited men and boats from islands around New Providence prior to launching their attack.[83] On April 18, the Spanish surrendered the Bahamas to Andrew Deveaux and his militia.[84] Deveaux's expedition was well received by the Crown. Brigadier General Archibald McArthur considered it "a very splendid action lately performed by Major Deveaux of the Beaufort militia."[85] Commissioners examining the loyalist claims gave Deveaux an annual allowance of one hundred pounds for his actions, "an act of Spirit which we admire and which we think ought not to go unrewarded."[86]

The adventurers who partook in the expedition were the first loyalists granted land in the newly acquired Bahamas. None won more than Deveaux himself. He gained 250 acres of land in Eastern New Providence, accompanied by another 1,000 acres on Cat Island.[87] His status as a landowner on the islands was thus established long before any loyalist refugees began to resettle there in 1784 and 1785, and he continued to buy Bahamas land throughout his life. Deveaux did not choose to reside on the islands, however, instead preferring a life in New York where he married and raised a family. By the time of his death in July 1812, in Red Hook, New York, Deveaux had sold off much of his Bahamas lands but in his will left 420 acres on eastern New Providence, 430 acres on the island of Highborn Cay, 340 acres on the islands of Little San Salvador, and 1,380 acres between Red Pond, Boatswain Hill, and Cat Island.[88] Andrew Deveaux's expedition to the Bahamas was one of the last military actions of the American Revolutionary War. It is significant because it effectively took the Bahamas away from the Spanish even though, unbeknownst to Deveaux, they had already been turned over to the British in the peace preliminaries.

On June 27, 1784, Spanish governor Manuel de Zespedes arrived in St. Augustine to officially take over East Florida's administration.[89] Bernardo de Galvez appointed Zespedes the governor of East Florida.[90] Zespedes reached St. Augustine with five hundred soldiers and government officials in thirteen ships.[91] Tonyn and Zespedes agreed that on July 12, 1784, the transfer of the Castillo de San Marcos marked the formal end to the British period in East Florida.[92] A ball commemorated the transfer of power.[93] Two days after taking power, Zespedes proclaimed that British subjects would be allowed to remain in East Florida provided they become Spanish subjects and convert to the Catholic religion. British subjects who did not agree to those terms would be forced to sell their property and leave.[94] While Zespedes got his administration in order, Tonyn remained in East Florida so he could work out a few issues arising from the Spanish transfer. Tonyn mostly dealt with property disputes, slave thefts, gangsters, and controversies.[95] From Zespedes's arrival until Tonyn's departure, East Florida was administered by two governments: the British and the Spanish. This dual governorship contributed to East Florida's chaotic final years as a British province. Until Britain's evacuation from East Florida was complete, no Spanish subject was allowed to travel to that province.[96]

By August 1785, Tonyn concluded his business in East

Florida.[97] The last British vessel departed East Florida from the mouth of the St. Marys River on November 19, 1785.[98] British soldiers protected and oversaw the evacuation process for departing loyalists.[99] Many loyalists embarked on evacuation vessels at the town of Hillsborough, now known as Old Town Fernandina, on Amelia Island.[100] Some loyalists dismantled their entire homes, intending to store the materials on board the evacuation ships. The ship captains refused to bring aboard entire houses, however, since they did not have sufficient room to store them. As far as animals were concerned, hogs and fowls were allowed on board, but horses and livestock were not. Refused horses and cattle were turned loose in the woods. Slaves took advantage of the chaos and ran away. Some slaves were stolen.[101] According to one passenger, the evacuation transports were crowded. People shared living space with cattle.[102] Tonyn arrived at Portsmouth, England, on January 11, 1786, aboard the *Two Sisters*.[103]

An uncounted many of the loyalist exodus from East Florida went into the North American interior, while 281 went to Europe (mostly Great Britain), 800 to Nova Scotia, 910 to Jamaica, 669 to Dominica, 3,247 to the Bahamas, 3,023 to the United States proper, and 278 to other foreign places most likely within the British Empire.[104] Most of the loyalists returning to England barely managed to get by. Many did not prosper there like they did in Florida. Practicing lawyers in East Florida who migrated to Britain were not admitted to the English bar. Without Spain's permission, several loyalists who fled into the North American interior, mainly former British Indian agents and people with mixed blood, went on to live in Florida with the Indians. Loyalist merchants also remained behind to engage in the Indian trade. The Panton, Leslie & Company, a company made up of former loyalists who traded with the Indians during the American Revolution, established a monopoly under the Spanish after 1783. Warehouses in the Bahamas supplied Florida's Indian goods for years after the war. Some Tories remained behind in the United States, Spanish Florida, or the West Indies because they waited to see what became of the newly formed United States of America. These loyalists believed the United States would fail after which Britain would restore its dominion over North America. These loyalists wanted to be close to their former homes when they returned under the restoration of British governance.[105]

In the American Revolutionary War narrative, loyalists have been dubbed the losers. Indeed, many loyalists lost valuable estates and property because of their allegiance to the Crown. To reward their loyalty, Parliament established the Parliamentary Commission for Enquiring into the Losses, Services, and Claims of the American Loyalists.[106] This committee looked into the various claims submitted by loyalists whose reports detailed the losses individuals, families, and estates incurred during the Revolutionary War. Each individual case was reviewed and assessed accordingly. Commissioners demanded evidence manifested in documentation or oral testimony for all claims. Unsupported claims, unattached to any evidence, were rejected.[107] In 1785 and 1787 Parliament set up the East Florida Claims Office to compensate East Florida loyalists for losses incurred in the transfer of that colony to Spain. From 1787 to 1789, the East Florida Claims Office processed 372 claims. Usually, the claimants received far less than what they requested. In East Florida overall, "a total of £647,405/6/9 was claimed" but only "£170,351/11/0 was awarded."[108] In addition to financial compensation, loyalists were granted free land in other dominions within the British Empire and jobs to boot.[109] Of the £18,347 Tonyn claimed, he received only £5,919. Successful claimants were paid in annuities and did not receive single lump-sum payments for their losses.[110]

Spain continued Britain's legacy of splitting Florida's administration in two. The Spaniards also continued British policy of reserving lands west of the St. Johns for the Native Americans.[111] In 1821, Florida was officially ceded to the United States. Patrick Tonyn remained in London for the rest of his life. He was promoted to colonel in 1777 and major general in 1781. He eventually died at the age of seventy-nine on December 30, 1804.[112] For the loyalists who returned to the United States, their part in the Revolutionary War would, in time, be forgiven and forgotten.[113] Some of the more violent men, like Thomas Brown and the East Florida Rangers, however, could not be forgiven. The damages they inflicted on the rebels during the war permanently shattered any hope they would otherwise have had for returning to their old communities. Most East Florida Rangers resettled in the British Empire while some attempted to return to Georgia. Many Revolutionary War veterans fought their return, claiming they had no right to come back. Throughout the war, roughly 1,200 to 1,500 men served in the East Florida Rangers. Of that number, 500 died and many of the rest were seriously injured. Thomas Brown resettled in the Bahamas and retired a well-off sugar planter.

Fate inevitably granted Brown his revenge, albeit indirectly, on one of the men who attacked him in 1775. In August 1782, a band of Creek warriors shot Thomas Graham in his house, one of Brown's 1775 assailants. During the War of 1812, Brown notified British officials that he was once again ready to take up his post as Superintendent of Indian Affairs in the southern district. He was keen to restore British authority to the Floridas. Despite his intentions, he never got that post.[114]

In total, East Florida's British period lasted twenty years—twenty-two if you count the settling of affairs, evacuation, and departure of the last British subjects. East Florida's role in the American Revolution was not only confined to the frontier space between East Florida and Georgia. East Florida soldiers participated in many wartime actions. East Florida troops participated in engagements in Georgia at Savannah, Augusta, White House, and Briar Creek; in South Carolina at Camden, Hanging Rock, and Musgrove Mills; and in Virginia at Petersburg. According to James Raab, Florida troops were also present at many skirmishes and battles leading up to the Battle of Yorktown. East Florida forces also defeated Francis Marion, known as the "Swamp Fox," twice, once at Cooper River and then again at the Santee River.[115]

Looking back, the Revolutionary War had a profound influence and impact on East Florida. Charles Mowat claims that the war cut short East Florida's growth.[116] Certainly, American raids decimated civilizing progress along East Florida's wild northern border. Had the war been avoided, East Florida's steady growth would have likely continued. Perhaps, in time, St. Augustine would have become a major port city like Savannah or Charleston. This idea seems highly plausible; after all, the British did more for East Florida's development than the Spanish had ever done prior to 1763. Continued efforts to settle East Florida, over time, would have delivered a flourishing colony that expanded into the Florida interior. The Revolutionary War, then, squashed East Florida's potential.

However, perhaps East Florida's deliverance from Britain was good for that province. When you get right down to it, British Parliamentarians cared little for East Florida. Unhappy about its acquisition in 1763 and quick to unload it in the peace preliminaries of 1782, British leaders in London did not value East Florida like they did their sugar plantations in the West Indies or their more developed colonies on the North American mainland. Perhaps, if Britain had kept East Florida after 1783, sometime down the road, East Florida's growth would have turned heads in Parliament. Parliamentarians would then have had no choice but to acknowledge that colony's contributions to the empire. Alas, that day never came. East Florida's period as a British province had come and gone.

With the passage of time, the British presence in East Florida became nothing more than a memory. During its tenure, East Florida existed on the fringes of the British Empire. Today British East Florida also exists on a fringe, only instead of a literal empire with defined spaces, it exists on a metaphorical fringe. Today, East Florida lives on along the fringes of contemporary American Revolution narratives, if it is mentioned at all. East Florida's relegation to this status is unfair. Wartime politics influenced and affected East Florida in more ways than one. Militias were raised, a general assembly was postponed,

St. Augustine experienced a heightened British troop presence, planters between the St. Johns and St. Marys Rivers suffered at the hands of Georgian raiding parties, and a constant threat of a Spanish or American invasion kept East Floridians on edge throughout the entire conflict. As this book has thus far demonstrated, between 1775 and 1783, three rebel invasions of East Florida solidified that province's role in the American War of Independence.

Conclusion

After 1783, numerous Florida Indian leaders traveled to London and petitioned King George III to regain possession of Florida. They wanted the king to guarantee the security of Native lands, something that was now gone after Britain's departure from the region.[1] As Kathleen DuVal points out, the aftermath of the American War of Independence set into motion events that eventually forced North American Indians, especially the Florida Seminoles, to contend with only one imperial power: the United States. The 1783 Treaty of Paris was the beginning of the end for the North American Indian way of life as unchecked white settler expansion poured into Indian Country. In prerevolutionary North America, Native American groups played off contending imperial powers. Pledging neutrality provided Native groups with independence. Subsequently, they were not subject to the demands of a single authority. If they did not like the conditions in one camp, they just migrated to the other. This diplomatic strategy of self-preservation was characteristic of Indian policy during the North American imperial wars. By the 1800s, southern Indian tribes were forced to deal with the terms of one authority: the United States, whose independence "was built on refusing to share the continent with empires or with sovereign Indians."[2]

In the end, Britain would never again formally possess territory in Florida. Some English-speaking East Floridians evacuated with the British and then returned later to play a role in the history of that region. Prominent examples include James Grant Forbes, William Augustus Bowles, and Zephaniah Kingsley Jr.

Forbes was born in St. Augustine in 1769. He evacuated with the British but returned to St. Augustine in 1821 as the first United States marshal. He would eventually become St. Augustine's mayor. Forbes went on to influence the "Forbes Purchase," which encompasses the modern-day Apalachicola National Forest.[3]

Bowles was a refugee from Maryland.[4] He became an ensign for the British and fought in West Florida at the Siege of Pensacola where he was almost blown up when the Queen's Redoubt exploded.[5] After West Florida's fall to the Spanish, Bowles relocated to the Bahamas where he secured orders from Bahamian governor Lord Dunmore to open up trade between the Bahamas and Florida Indians.[6] Instead of obeying his orders, Bowles raised an army of sixty men, including loyalists, sailors, and convicts and sailed for Florida. In April 1788, two armed schooners landed Bowles's force at the Mosquito Inlet.[7] Dressed in a gold-laced British uniform, Bowles sought to make Florida a British colony or protectorate once again.[8] He called it the independent "State of Muskogee." Bowles and his force moved inland to destroy an Indian trading post near Lake George.[9] Bowles's army struggled as they carried their heavy swivel guns and blunderbusses through the thick Florida woods and swamps.[10] When the Spaniards caught wind of this attack, a party of Spanish soldiers marched from St. Augustine to intercept Bowles and his men. Repelled at the prospect of a heated engagement, Bowles abandoned his Lake George plans and traveled north to the Indian town of Cuscowilla, in Alachua. At Cuscowilla, Bowles's expedition fell apart. His men deserted him, and the Indians refused to enlist in his army. After this failure, Bowles attempted to exert his influence over the Creeks. He was more successful there. Claiming to be a British agent, Bowles convinced many Creek chiefs to seize various trading houses.[11] He remained with the Creeks during the winter of 1788–1789, eventually returning to the Bahamas to regroup. In October 1790, Bowles traveled to London to enlist support from the British government. When he reached London, Bowles proclaimed himself "Ambassador from the United Nations of Creeks, and Cherokees, to the Court of London." In January 1791, Bowles laid out his plan to recapture Florida before Lord Grenville. He asked for arms and military stores. He received neither. He returned to Florida in 1791. The flag of the "Muskogee nation" flew over the ship he sailed back to Florida.[12]

For the next decade, Bowles refused to relinquish his aspirations for an independent state of Muskogee. In all his adventures, the most significant was his military success at Fort St. Mark. In 1800, Bowles led a force of Creeks to the St. Marks River and captured the armed trading vessel *Sheerwater*.[13] Assisted by Seminole warriors, Bowles captured Fort St. Mark after a one-month siege on May 19, 1800. Bowles held this position for three weeks until he was forced to flee in late June after Spanish troops arrived from Pensacola.[14] While Bowles managed to

Painting of William Augustus Bowles, 1790 (State Archives of Florida).

get away, the Spaniards put a six-thousand-dollar bounty on his head.[15] Between 1800 and 1801, Bowles armed privateers out of the Bahamas to serve in the Muskogee navy. Eventually, Bowles was captured in May 1803.[16] The Creeks turned him in to Spanish authorities. Bowles was sent to Madrid. He was released on the condition that he return to Europe. Ignoring the conditions of his parole, Bowles immediately headed to Florida and resumed his operations of conquering that territory. In 1804, the Spanish captured him once again. This time he was sent to Havana where he died in December 1805.[17]

Kingsley fled Charleston with his family at the end of the Revolution and likely resided in East Florida before relocating to Canada and then the West Indies. He returned to East Florida in 1803. He then founded a plantation on Fort George Island near the mouth of the St. Johns River. Today, the Kingsley Plantation is a historic site that draws tourists from all around the state. Further south, East Florida refugees and their descendants were the first permanent settlers of the Florida Keys.[18]

Today, traces of British East Florida are hard to find. The smaller East Florida towns like Cowford, Rollestown, Hillsborough, and St. Johns Bluff have all disappeared. The East Florida settlements that existed during the eighteenth century are overgrown and hard to locate. Only the location of Andrew Turnbull's New Smyrna plantation can be readily identified. The coquina foundation of that settlement's plantation house resides in what is now the town of New Smyrna Beach. Further north, the St. Marys boundary between Florida and Georgia was established by the British.[19] That boundary line is still observed to this day. Apart from the lesser-known traces of British East Florida, the legacy and memory of that province is extensive. Three editions of the *East Florida Gazette* can be accessed by anyone online. The original copies reside in the British National Archives in Kew, outside London, England. Photocopies are available at the Library of Congress and State Archives of Florida. Two historical fiction books take place in East Florida. Stephen Vincent Benet's *Spanish Bayonet* (1926) tells the tale of his Minorcan ancestors from East Florida both before and after the Revolutionary War. Eugenia Price's *Maria* (1977) tells the tale of Mary Evans and her life in St. Augustine during the British colonial period. Several historical markers continue to remind and educate the public about East Florida's connection to the American Revolution. These markers can be found in Old Town Fernandina, Fernandina Beach, Callahan, Jacksonville, and St. Augustine.

East Florida's significance in the American Revolution lies in that province's contributions to the British Empire. East Florida served as a barrier colony, protecting the British West Indies from the spread of rebellion; stood as a haven for loyalists fleeing wartime persecution; supplied raw materials to West Indian markets; and threatened Georgia's security. East Florida's presence diverted much needed resources away from the rebellion to the East Florida–Georgia border. Additionally, East Florida also played an important role in the southern theater where two major battles and countless small skirmishes were fought. Contemporary scholarship's failure to cover British East Florida in the American Revolution does not suggest that the province was unimportant. Far from it. Such a lack of coverage is a reminder for scholars to emphasize East Florida's presence in the war that made America.

Notes

INTRODUCTION

1 George Washington to Brigadier General Robert Howe, March 17, 1777, *Founders Online*, National Archives, https://founders.archives.gov/documents/Washington/03-08-02-0633.

2 Dr. Roger Smith, *The 14th Colony: The American Revolution's Best Kept Secret* (St. Augustine: Colonial Research Associates, 2011), 2. Those thirty-three colonies were: Virginia, Massachusetts, Maryland, New Hampshire, Rhode Island, Connecticut, New York, New Jersey, Pennsylvania, Delaware, North Carolina, South Carolina, Georgia, East Florida, West Florida, Quebec, Nova Scotia, St. Johns Island, Newfoundland, Bermuda, Jamaica, Saint Christopher, Antigua, Barbuda, British Virgin Islands, Montserrat, Nevis, Anguilla, the settlement of Belize in British Honduras, Mosquito Coast, Bay Islands, Cayman Islands, and the British Windward Islands. Britain also possessed various territories by 1775 that had not yet been officially colonized. Those included: Rupert's Land, the British Arctic Territories, and the Indian Reserve (often referred to as Indian Country).

3 Daniel L. Schafer, "Chapter Eight: Of Engineers and Cartographers," *El Escribano: The St. Augustine Journal of History: St. Augustine's British Years 1763–1784* 38 (2001), 115–116; Mark F. Boyd, "A Map of the Road from Pensacola to St. Augustine, 1778," *The Florida Historical Quarterly* 17 (July 1938), 1: 15–23.

4 For more books on British East Florida see: Wilbur Henry Siebert's *Loyalists in East Florida: 1774–1785* (1929), Burton Barrs's *East Florida in the American Revolution* (1932), and Charles Loch Mowat's *East Florida as a British Province, 1763–1784* (1943). To this day, Mowat's book is the most thorough and detailed account of East Florida's British colonial period. The Florida Bicentennial Commission published J. Leitch Wright Jr.'s *Florida in the American Revolution* (1975), *British St. Augustine* (1975), *Eighteenth-Century Florida and Its Borderlands* (1975), *Eighteenth-Century Florida and the Caribbean* (1976),

Eighteenth-Century Florida: Life on the Frontier (1976), *Eighteenth-Century Florida and the Revolutionary South* (1978), and *Eighteenth-Century Florida: The Impact of the American Revolution* (1978). The 1980s and 1990s produced Martha Condray Searcy's *The Georgia-Florida Contest in the American Revolution, 1776–1778* (1985), Edward J. Cashin's *The King's Ranger: Thomas Brown and the American Revolution on The Southern Frontier* (1989), and Paul David Nelson's *General James Grant: Scottish Soldier and Royal Governor of East Florida* (1993). In 2001, an edition of *El Escribano: The St. Augustine Journal of History* published "St. Augustine's British Years 1763–1784," (2001). In 2008, James W. Raab published *Spain, Britain and the American Revolution in Florida, 1763–1783* (2008). The 2010s witnessed the publication of Dr. Roger Smith's *The 14th Colony: The American Revolution's Best Kept Secret* (2011).

5 Samuel Proctor, ed., *Eighteenth-Century Florida and the Caribbean* (Gainesville: University Presses of Florida, 1976), vii.

6 Daniel Baugh, *The Global Seven Years' War 1754–1763* (New York: Routledge, 2014), 559–619.

7 Charles Loch Mowat, *East Florida as a British Province, 1763–1784* (1943; reprint, London: Forgotten Books, 2018), 5.

8 S. Max Edelson, *The New Map of Empire: How Britain Imagined America Before Independence* (Cambridge: Harvard University Press, 2017), 38–63.

9 Mowat, *East Florida as a British Province*, 5.

10 Smith, *The 14th Colony*, 4.

11 Smith, *The 14th Colony*, 4.

12 *The Parliamentary History of England, from the Earliest Period to the Year 1803* (London: R. Bagshaw, 1813), 15: 1264.

13 Horace Walpole, *Memoirs of the Reign of King George III* (London: Lawrence and Bullen, 1894), 1: 221; Paul E. Hoffman, *Florida's Frontiers* (Bloomington: Indiana University Press, 2002), 208. Bagshot Heath is a bog in Surrey, England.

14 Hoffman, *Florida's Frontiers*, 208.

15 Edelson, *The New Map of Empire*, 59; Colin G. Calloway, *The Scratch of a Pen: 1763 and the Transformation of North America* (New York: Oxford University Press, 2006), 92–100.

16 Edward J. Cashin, *Governor Henry Ellis and the Transformation of British North America* (Athens: University of Georgia Press, 1994), 185–186.

17 Calloway, *The Scratch of a Pen*, 56–59, 92–100.

18 Sketch of Propositions for a Peace, [after 26 September 1776 and before October 25, 1776], *Founders Online*, National Archives, https://founders.archives.gov/documents/Franklin/01–22-02–0372.

CHAPTER ONE. BRITISH EAST FLORIDA

1 Mark VanDoren, ed., *Travels of William Bartram* (New York: Dover Publications, 1955), 75–79, 94–96. Bartram's original book was published in 1791 under the title, *Travels Through North & South Carolina, Georgia, East & West Florida, The Cherokee Country, The Extensive Territories of the Muscogulges or Creek confederacy, and the Country of the Chactaws.*

2 Wright Jr., *Florida in the American Revolution*, 99–100.

3 Mowat, *East Florida as a British Province*, 7–8; David P. Henige, *Colonial Governors from the Fifteenth Century to the Present* (Madison: University of Wisconsin Press, 1970), 297.

4 Hoffman, *Florida's Frontiers*, 209–210.

5 Daniel L. Schafer, "Chapter One: 'not an herb, not a cabbage, all is overgrown with weeds,'" *El Escribano: The St. Augustine Journal of History: St. Augustine's British Years 1763–1784* 38 (2001): 12.

6 Paul David Nelson, *General James Grant: Scottish Soldier and Royal Governor of East Florida* (Gainesville: University Press of Florida, 1993), 3–4, 7–8, 17–29, 30–44, 47.

7 Mowat, *East Florida as a British Province*, 14.

8 Daniel L. Schafer, "Chapter Five: Governing the Town," *El Escribano: The St. Augustine Journal of History: St. Augustine's British Years 1763–1784* 38 (2001): 50.

9 Mowat, *East Florida as a British Province*, 16.

10 J. Leitch. Wright Jr. *British St. Augustine* (St. Augustine: Historic St. Augustine Preservation Board, 1975), 5; Mowat, *East Florida as a British Province*, 17. Albert Manucy, "Changing Traditions in St. Augustine Architecture," In E*ighteenth-Century Florida: The Impact of the American Revolution*, edited by Samuel Proctor (Gainesville: University Presses of Florida, 1978), 116.

11 Wright Jr. *British St. Augustine*, 5.

12 Daniel L. Schafer, "Chapter Five: Governing the Town," *El Escribano: The St. Augustine Journal of History: St. Augustine's British Years 1763–1784* 38 (2001): 52.

13 Wright Jr. *British St. Augustine*, 5.

14 J. Leitch Wright Jr., *Florida in the American Revolution* (Gainesville: University Press of Florida, 1975), 14.
15 Mowat, *East Florida as a British Province*, 17.
16 Wright Jr. *British St. Augustine*, 4–5.
17 Wright Jr., *Florida in the American Revolution*, 14.
18 Wright Jr. *British St. Augustine*, 2.
19 Luis Rafael Arana, "The Basis of a Permanent Fortification," *El Escribano: The St. Augustine Journal of History: Defenses and Defenders at St. Augustine* 36 (1999): 3–10.
20 Luis Rafael Arana, "Governor Cendoya's Negotiations in Mexico for a Stone Fort in St. Augustine," *El Escribano: The St. Augustine Journal of History: Defenses and Defenders at St. Augustine* 36 (1999): 22, 25–26, 28.
21 Luis Rafael Arana, "Don Manuel de Cendoya and Castillo de San Marcos, 1669–1673," *El Escribano: The St. Augustine Journal of History: Defenses and Defenders at St. Augustine* 36 (1999): 35.
22 Wright Jr. *British St. Augustine*, 2; Luis Rafael Arana, "Construction at Castillo de San Marcos," *El Escribano: The St. Augustine Journal of History: Defenses and Defenders at St. Augustine* 36 (1999): 119.
23 James W. Raab, *Spain, Britain and the American Revolution in Florida, 1763–1783* (Jefferson: McFarland & Company, 2008), 12.
24 Mowat, *East Florida as a British Province*, 17–18.
25 Wright Jr. *British St. Augustine*, 2.
26 Wright Jr. *British St. Augustine*, 2.
27 Luis Rafael Arana, "The Cubo Line, 1704–1909," *El Escribano: The St. Augustine Journal of History: Defenses and Defenders at St. Augustine* 36 (1999): 187–188.
28 Wright Jr. *British St. Augustine*, 2.
29 Arana, "The Cubo Line, 1704–1909," 187–188.
30 The Rosario Defense Line Marker, St. Augustine, Florida 32084. 29° 53.799' N, 81° 18.885' in St. Johns County. According to the Historical Marker Database, the marker is on Cordova Street, on the right when traveling north. Marker is in this post office area.
31 Rosario Defense Line Marker.
32 Raab, *Spain, Britain and the American Revolution in Florida, 1763–1783*, 12.
33 Mowat, *East Florida as a British Province*, 26.
34 Hoffman, *Florida's Frontiers*, 226.
35 Wright Jr., *Florida in the American Revolution*, 106.
36 Governor Patrick Tonyn to Lord George Germain, December 9,

1780, K. G. Davies, *Documents of the American Revolution, 1770–1783* (Colonial Office Series) (Dublin: Irish University Press, 1978), 18: 252–255.

37 Daniel L. Schafer, "Chapter Thirteen: A 'secure Asylum,'" *El Escribano: The St. Augustine Journal of History: St. Augustine's British Years 1763–1784* 38 (2001): 225.

38 Hoffman, *Florida's Frontiers*, 226.

39 Schafer, "Chapter Thirteen," 224–228.

40 Wright Jr., *Florida in the American Revolution*, 106.

41 Wright Jr., *Florida in the American Revolution*, 106–107.

42 Mowat, *East Florida as a British Province*, 18–20.

43 Raab, *Spain, Britain and the American Revolution in Florida, 1763–1783*, 28.

44 Wright Jr., *Florida in the American Revolution*, 7, 12.

45 James H. O'Donnell III, "The Florida Revolutionary Indian Frontier: Abode of the Blessed or Field of Battle?" In *Eighteenth-Century Florida: Life on the Frontier*, edited by Samuel Proctor (Gainesville: University Presses of Florida, 1976), 60–61.

46 Mowat, *East Florida as a British Province*, 20–21.

47 Daniel L. Schafer, "Chapter Seven: An Evolving Indian Policy," *El Escribano: The St. Augustine Journal of History: St. Augustine's British Years 1763–1784* 38 (2001): 78–79.

48 Wright Jr., *Florida in the American Revolution*, 7; William S. Coker, "Entrepreneurs in the British and Spanish Floridas, 1775–1821," In *Eighteenth-Century Florida and the Caribbean*, edited by Samuel Proctor (Gainesville: University Presses of Florida, 1976), 15–39.

49 Schafer, "Chapter Seven," 87–88, 95–96.

50 Oliver Morton Dickerson, *American Colonial Government 1696–1765: A study of the British Board of Trade in its relation to the American Colonies, Political, Industrial, Administrative* (Cleveland: The Arthur H. Clark Company, 1912), 158–159.

51 Jack P. Greene, "The Role of the Lower Houses of Assembly in Eighteenth-Century Politics," *The Journal of Southern History* 27, no. 4 (November 1961): 453–454.

52 Mowat, *East Florida as a British Province*, 34, 40, 42–43.

53 David R. Chesnutt, "South Carolina's Impact upon East Florida, 1763–1776," In *Eighteenth-Century Florida and the Revolutionary South*, edited by Samuel Proctor (Gainesville: University Presses of Florida, 1978), 5–14.

54 Mowat, *East Florida as a British Province*, 50–52.

55 Raab, *Spain, Britain and the American Revolution in Florida, 1763–1783*, 23–24.

56 Daniel L. Schafer, "Early Plantation Development in British East Florida," *El Escribano: The St. Augustine Journal of History* 19 (1982): 47.

57 Louis De Vorsey Jr., "De Brahm's East Florida on the Eve of Revolution: The Materials for Its Re-creation." In *Eighteenth-Century Florida and Its Borderlands*, edited by Samuel Proctor (Gainesville: University Presses of Florida, 1975), 86; Mowat, *East Florida as a British Province*, 52–53.

58 Mowat, *East Florida as a British Province*, 54.

59 Mowat, *East Florida as a British Province*, 54–55, 58–59.

60 Schafer, "Early Plantation Development in British East Florida," 46; Daniel L. Schafer, "Chapter Nine: 'A sensible Clever man'-The Rise and Fall of Andrew Turnbull," *El Escribano: The St. Augustine Journal of History: St. Augustine's British Years 1763–1784* 38 (2001): 118. For more on the East Florida Society see George C. Rogers Jr.'s "The East Florida Society of London," *The Florida Historical Quarterly* 54, no. 4 (April 1976): 479–496.

61 Schafer, "Early Plantation Development in British East Florida," 37, 41–42.

62 Mowat, *East Florida as a British Province*, 69.

63 Daniel L. Schafer, "Chapter Three: 'till this new world has in some means been created,'" *El Escribano: The St. Augustine Journal of History: St. Augustine's British Years 1763–1784* 38 (2001): 28–40; Mowat, *East Florida as a British Province*, 68–69. Planters and overseers regularly visited Grant's plantation to observe his methods of cultivating and manufacturing indigo weed and dye (Raab, 27–28). For more information on James Grant's plantation see Daniel L. Schafer's "Governor James Grant's Villa: A British East Florida Indigo Plantation," *El Escribano: The St. Augustine Journal of History* 37 (2000): 1-120.

64 Wright Jr., *Florida in the American Revolution*, 13. The demise of Andrew Turnbull's New Smyrna colony is one example of a failed East Florida plantation. Wealthy philanthropist Denys Rolle tried unsuccessfully in his initial attempts early on to establish a plantation, called Rollestown or Rolle Town, in East Florida along the east bank of the St. Johns River. Suffering numerous setbacks, Rolle was forced to abandon his East Florida plans, returning later in 1778 to find success with the 150 black field hands he brought with him. For more on Denys Rolle see Carita Doggett Corse and James Grant's, "Denys Rolle and Rollestown,

a Pioneer for Utopia," *The Florida Historical Society Quarterly* 7, no. 2 (October 1928): 115–134; Charles L. Mowat's, "The Tribulations of Denys Rolle," *The Florida Historical Quarterly* 23, no. 1 (July 1944): 1–14; and Claude C. Sturgill's, ed., *The Humble Petition of Denys Rolle, Esq; setting forth the Hardships, Inconveniencies, and Grievances, which have attended him in his Attempts to make a Settlement in East Florida, humbly praying such Relief, as in their Lordships Wisdom shall seem meet, 1765* (Gainesville: University Presses of Florida, 1977).

65 Lieutenant Governor John Moultrie to Earl of Dartmouth, May 16, 1773, K. G. Davies, ed., *Documents of the American Revolution, 1770–1783 (Colonial Office Series)* (Dublin: Irish University Press, 1974), 6: 146–147.

66 Mowat, *East Florida as a British Province*, 59–61, 65.

67 Bernard Bailyn, *Voyagers to the West: A Passage in the Peopling of America on the Eve of the Revolution* (New York: Alfred A. Knopf, 1986), 430–474.

68 Schafer, "Chapter Three: 'till this new world has in some means been created,'" 39.

69 Mowat, *East Florida as a British Province*, 67.

70 Pleasant Daniel Gold, *History of Duval County Including Early History of East Florida* (St. Augustine: The Record Company, 1929), 51.

71 Daniel L. Schafer, "Chapter Ten: Acting Governor John Moultrie," *El Escribano: The St. Augustine Journal of History: St. Augustine's British Years 1763–1784* 38 (2001): 168.

72 Gold, *History of Duval County Including Early History of East Florida*, 53.

73 Mowat, *East Florida as a British Province*, 68.

74 Wright Jr., *Florida in the American Revolution*, 4–5.

75 Mowat, *East Florida as a British Province*, 78.

76 Wright Jr., *Florida in the American Revolution*, 14.

77 Samuel P. Turner, "Maritime Insights from St. Augustine's British Period," *El Escribano: The St. Augustine Journal of History* 47 (2010): 20–21.

78 Daniel L. Schafer, "Chapter Two: 'Peopling & settling the new Established Colonies,'" *El Escribano: The St. Augustine Journal of History: St. Augustine's British Years 1763–1784* 38 (2001): 24–25.

79 Daniel L. Schafer, "Chapter Four: 'sharers of the wicked bottle,'" *El Escribano: The St. Augustine Journal of History: St. Augustine's British Years 1763–1784* 38 (2001): 41–47; Raab, *Spain, Britain and the American Revolution in Florida, 1763–1783*, 23.

80 Daniel L. Schafer, "Chapter Six: The Royal Botanist and the St. Johns River," *El Escribano: The St. Augustine Journal of History: St. Augustine's British Years 1763–1784* 38 (2001): 65. In addition to dinner parties, Grant contributed further to East Florida's social scene by founding East Florida's Masonic Lodge where he was appointed Grand Master (Raab, 31). Privately, Grant and a small circle of close friends met regularly at his house to drink (Raab, 31).

81 Jim Piecuch, "Patrick Tonyn: Britain's Most Effective Revolutionary-Era Royal Governor," *Journal of the American Revolution*, March 22, 2018, https://allthingsliberty.com/2018/03/patrick-tonyn-britains-most-effective-revolutionary-era-royal-governor/; Mowat, East Florida as a *British Province*, 83.

82 Piecuch, "Patrick Tonyn: Britain's Most Effective Revolutionary-Era Royal Governor."

83 Daniel L. Schafer, "Chapter Eleven: Men at Odds," *El Escribano: The St. Augustine Journal of History: St. Augustine's British Years 1763–1784* 38 (2001): 178.

84 Mowat, *East Florida as a British Province*, 83–85; Wright Jr., *Florida in the American Revolution*, 17.

85 Hoffman, *Florida's Frontiers*, 223.

86 Wright Jr., *Florida in the American Revolution*, 17–18.

87 Hoffman, *Florida's Frontiers*, 223.

88 Wright Jr., *Florida in the American Revolution*, 99.

89 J. Leitch Wright, "British East Florida: Loyalist Bastion," In *Eighteenth-Century Florida: The Impact of the American Revolution*, edited by Samuel Proctor (Gainesville: University Presses of Florida, 1978), 7; Wright Jr., *Florida in the American Revolution*, 21; also see Linda K. Williams, "East Florida as a Loyalist Haven," *The Florida Historical Quarterly* 54, no. 4 (April 1976): 465–478.

90 Hoffman, *Florida's Frontiers*, 228–229.

91 Raab, *Spain, Britain and the American Revolution in Florida, 1763–1783*, 104.

92 Wright Jr., *Florida in the American Revolution*, 21–23.

93 Wilbur Henry Siebert, *Loyalists in East Florida, 1774–1785* (1929; reprint, Greenville: Southern Historical Press), 1: 23–24.

94 Schafer, "Chapter Thirteen," 207; Siebert, *Loyalists in East Florida, 1774–1785*, 1: 95.

95 Governor Patrick Tonyn to Earl of Shelburne, November 14, 1782, K. G. Davies, *Documents of the American Revolution, 1770–1783 (Colonial Office Series)* (Dublin: Irish University Press, 1981), 21: 136–137.

96 Daniel L. Schafer, "Chapter Fourteen: The Fate of East Florida," *El Escribano: The St. Augustine Journal of History: St. Augustine's British Years 1763–1784* 38 (2001), 234.

97 Schafer, "Chapter Fourteen," 237.

98 Schafer, "Chapter Thirteen," 207, 218. Sometime before February 22, 1783, some East Floridian bakers and bread sellers were found guilty of selling overpriced bread. British officials attempted to curb the exploitation of East Florida's inhabitants (particularly needy refugees) by fixing a monthly quality, weight, and price for every bread loaf. Standards for the market price of flour and the weights of distinct sizes of bread were posted and updated monthly and subject to change. Justices, churchwardens, and vestrymen were given the authority to enter any house, shop, stall, bake-house, or ware-house belonging to any baker or seller of bread in East Florida and inspect the quality of however many bread loaves they desired. If the quality of the bread was deemed subpar, it was confiscated and donated to the poor (*East Florida Gazette*, Volume I Number 5, February 22 to March 1, 1783).

99 For more on African Americans of East Florida see J. Leitch Wright Jr.'s "Blacks in British East Florida," *The Florida Historical Quarterly* 54, no. 4 (April 1976): 425–442.

100 Dr. Roger Smith, *Hope of Freedom: Southern Blacks and the American Revolution* (St. Augustine: Colonial Research Associates, 2015), 15.

101 Smith, *Hope of Freedom*, 26.

102 Daniel L. Schafer, "Chapter Twelve: War on the Border," *El Escribano: The St. Augustine Journal of History: St. Augustine's British Years 1763–1784* 38 (2001), 199.

103 Wright Jr., *Florida in the American Revolution*, 108–109.

104 Mowat, *East Florida as a British Province*, 86; Wright Jr., *Florida in the American Revolution*, 16.

105 Worthington Chauncey Ford, ed., *Journals of the Continental Congress, 1774–1789* 1 (Washington: Government Printing Press, 1904), 101.

106 Raab, *Spain, Britain and the American Revolution in Florida, 1763–1783*, 81.

107 Wright Jr., *Florida in the American Revolution*, 17–19.

108 For further reading on the New Smyrna colony see: Carita Doggett Corse, *Dr. Andrew Turnbull and The New Smyrna Colony of Florida* (Florida: The Drew Press, 1919); Kenneth H. Beeson Jr., *Fromajadas and Indigo: The Minorcan Colony in Florida* (Charleston: The History Press, 2006); Epaminondas P. Panagopoulos, *New Smyrna: An Eighteenth Century Greek Odyssey* (Gainesville: University of Florida Press, 1966).

109 Bisset to Patrick Tonyn, September 1, 1776, Carita Doggett Corse, ed., *The Turnbull Papers* (Jacksonville, 1940), 158.
110 Wright Jr., *Florida in the American Revolution*, 104–105.
111 Governor Patrick Tonyn to Lord George Germain, April 2, 1776, K. G. Davies, *Documents of the American Revolution, 1770–1783 (Colonial Office Series)* (Dublin: Irish University Press, 1976), 12: 103–105.
112 Wright Jr., *Florida in the American Revolution*, 23.
113 Selwyn H. H. Carrington, "The American Revolution and the British West Indies' Economy," *The Journal of Interdisciplinary History* 17, no. 4 (Spring 1987): 827.
114 Richard B. Sheridan, "The British Sugar Planters and the Atlantic World, 1763–1775," In *Eighteenth-Century Florida and the Caribbean*, edited by Samuel Proctor (Gainesville: University Presses of Florida, 1976), 5.
115 Wright Jr., *Florida in the American Revolution*, 23–24; Governor Patrick Tonyn to Lord George Germain, October 30, 1776, Davies, *Documents of the American Revolution, 1770–1783*, 12: 243–244.
116 Worthington Chauncey Ford, ed., *Journals of the Continental Congress, 1774–1789* (Washington: Government Printing Press, 1905), 2: 54.
117 Wright Jr., *Florida in the American Revolution*, 27.
118 Wright Jr., *Florida in the American Revolution*, 24–26.
119 Wright, "British East Florida: Loyalist Bastion," 7.
120 William R. Nester, *The Frontier War for American Independence* (Mechanicsburg: Stackpole Books, 2004), 87.
121 Wright Jr., *Florida in the American Revolution*, 26.
122 Luis Rafael Arana, "British Regiments in St. Augusine, 1763–1784," *El Escribano: The St. Augustine Journal of History: Defenses and Defenders at St. Augustine* 36 (1999): 115.
123 Raab, *Spain, Britain and the American Revolution in Florida, 1763–1783*,75–76.
124 Arana, "British Regiments in St. Augustine, 1763–1784," 115; Mowat, *East Florida as a British Province*, 108.
125 Wright Jr., *Florida in the American Revolution*, 26.
126 Governor Patrick Tonyn to Earl of Dartmouth, July 1, 1775, K. G. Davies, ed., *Documents of the American Revolution, 1770–1783 (Colonial Office Series)* (Dublin: Irish University Press, 1976), 11: 30–32.
127 Wright Jr., *Florida in the American Revolution*, 28.
128 George E. Buker, and Richard Apley Martin, "Governor Tonyn's Brown-Water Navy: East Florida During the American Revolution, 1775–1778," *The Florida Historical Quarterly* 58, no. 1 (July 1979): 59.

129 Wright Jr., *Florida in the American Revolution*, 27.
130 Governor Patrick Tonyn to Earl of Dartmouth, August 24, 1775, Davies, *Documents of the American Revolution, 1770–1783*, 11: 84–85.
131 Wright Jr., *Florida in the American Revolution*, 27.
132 Buker and Martin, "Governor Tonyn's Brown-Water Navy," 60; Governor Patrick Tonyn to Earl of Dartmouth, August 24, 1775, Davies, *Documents of the American Revolution, 1770–1783*, 11: 84–85.
133 Wright Jr., *Florida in the American Revolution*, 30.
134 Siebert, *Loyalists in East Florida, 1774–1785*, 1: 30.
135 Smith, *The 14th Colony*, 16.
136 George Washington to John Hancock, December 18, 1775, *Founders Online*, National Archives, https://founders.archives.gov/documents/Washington/03–02-02–0528.
137 Wright Jr., *Florida in the American Revolution*, 65.

CHAPTER TWO. BORDER WARFARE AND THE FIRST AMERICAN INVASION OF EAST FLORIDA

1 Worthington Chauncey Ford, ed., *Journals of the Continental Congress, 1774–1789* (Washington: Government Printing Press, 1906), 4: 15.
2 Smith, *The 14th Colony*, 16.
3 Governor Patrick Tonyn to Lord George Germain, October 30, 1776, Davies, *Documents of the American Revolution, 1770–1783* (Dublin: Irish University Press, 1976), 12: 243–244.
4 Smith, *The 14th Colony*, 17.
5 Mowat, *East Florida as a British Province*, 107–109, 112.
6 Patrick Tonyn to Lord George Germain, August 21, 1776, *The On-Line Institute for Advanced Loyalist Studies*, transcribed by Todd Braisted, http://www.royalprovincial.com/military/rhist/eastflmil/eflmillet1.htm.
7 Raab, *Spain, Britain and the American Revolution in Florida, 1763–1783*, 83.
8 Patrick Tonyn to General Henry Clinton, April 15, 1776, *The On-Line Institute for Advanced Loyalist Studies*, transcribed by Todd Braisted, http://www.royalprovincial.com/military/rhist/eastfr/easttoni.htm; Mowat, East Florida as a British Province, 110. While some sources incorrectly claim the East Florida Rangers were founded in 1774, the East Florida Rangers did not receive official authorization for their founding until 1776. An unauthorized troop of Rangers was created in East Florida in 1774 during the Indian scare, but this corps cannot

be called the East Florida Rangers since they did not have official authorization from British officials (Searcy, 38).

9 Mowat, *East Florida as a British Province*, 110.

10 Martha Condray Searcy, *The Georgia-Florida Contest in the American Revolution, 1776–1778* (Tuscaloosa: University of Alabama Press, 1985), 83.

11 Raab, *Spain, Britain and the American Revolution in Florida, 1763–1783*, 84. 150 African Americans served in the East Florida Rangers throughout the Revolutionary War (Smith, *Hope of Freedom*, 30–31).

12 Governor Patrick Tonyn to Lord George Germain, October 30, 1776, Davies, *Documents of the American Revolution, 1770–1783* (Dublin: Irish University Press, 1976), 12: 243.

13 Mowat, *East Florida as a British Province*, 110–111. While Thomas Brown was commander of the East Florida Rangers, he answered to East Florida's Governor.

14 For more on the disputes over the authority of East Florida's Rangers see W. Calvin Smith's "Mermaids Riding Alligators: Divided Command on the Southern Frontier, 1776–1778," *The Florida Historical Quarterly* 54, no. 4 (April 1976): 443–464.

15 Schafer, "Chapter Twelve," 192.

16 Edward J. Cashin, *The King's Ranger: Thomas Brown and the American Revolution on the Southern Frontier* (Athens: University of Georgia Press, 1989), 1, 6–19, 27–29.

17 Raab, *Spain, Britain and the American Revolution in Florida, 1763–1783*, 85.

18 Cashin, *The King's Ranger*, 28–29, 40–41.

19 Mowat, *East Florida as a British Province*, 114.

20 Hoffman, *Florida's Frontiers*, 227.

21 Buker and Martin, "Governor Tonyn's Brown-Water Navy," 65.

22 Searcy, *The Georgia-Florida Contest in the American Revolution, 1776–1778*, 46; Mowat, *East Florida as a British Province*, 115.

23 Schafer, "Chapter Twelve," 191.

24 Disposition of H. M.'s Ships and Vessels in North America, November 5, 1776, Davies, *Documents of the American Revolution, 1770–1783* (Dublin: Irish University Press, 1976), 12: 244–246.

25 Mowat, *East Florida as a British Province*, 113.

26 Siebert, *Loyalists in East Florida, 1774–1785*, 1: 8–9, 41.

27 Seminole Chief Cowkeeper did not attend this meeting (Schafer, 196).

28 Schafer, "Chapter Twelve," 196–197.

29 Raab, *Spain, Britain and the American Revolution in Florida, 1763–1783*, 86.

30 Rachel B. Herrmann, *No Useless Mouth: Waging War and Fighting Hunger in the American Revolution* (Ithaca: Cornell University Press, 2019), 47.

31 Burton Barrs, *East Florida in the American Revolution* (Jacksonville: The Cooper Press, 1949), 6.

32 Helen Hornbeck Tanner, "Pipesmoke and Muskets: Florida Indian Intrigues of the Revolutionary Era," In *Eighteenth-Century Florida and Its Borderlands*, edited by Samuel Proctor (Gainesville: University Presses of Florida, 1975), 21.

33 Searcy, *The Georgia-Florida Contest in the American Revolution, 1776–1778*, 43; Raab, *Spain, Britain and the American Revolution in Florida, 1763–1783*, 86.

34 Wright Jr., *Florida in the American Revolution*, 38.

35 Siebert, *Loyalists in East Florida, 1774–1785*, 1: 37–39.

36 *Collections of the Georgia Historical Society* (Savannah: Braid & Hutton, Printers & Binders, 1901), 5: 51–52, 54.

37 Searcy, *The Georgia-Florida Contest in the American Revolution, 1776–1778*, 34–35.

38 Siebert, *Loyalists in East Florida, 1774–1785*, 1: 39.

39 Searcy, *The Georgia-Florida Contest in the American Revolution, 1776–1778*, 35–37, 44.

40 Wright Jr., *Florida in the American Revolution*, 38.

41 Searcy, *The Georgia-Florida Contest in the American Revolution, 1776–1778*, 37–38.

42 Searcy, *The Georgia-Florida Contest in the American Revolution, 1776–1778*, 43–45.

43 Searcy, *The Georgia-Florida Contest in the American Revolution, 1776–1778*, 46–50.

44 Searcy, *The Georgia-Florida Contest in the American Revolution, 1776–1778*, 50.

45 Barrs, *East Florida in the American Revolution*, 10.

46 Searcy, *The Georgia-Florida Contest in the American Revolution, 1776–1778*, 50.

47 *Collections of the Georgia Historical Society*, 5: 93.

48 Searcy, *The Georgia-Florida Contest in the American Revolution, 1776–1778*, 54–55.

49 *Collections of the Georgia Historical Society*, 5: 93–95.

50 Searcy, *The Georgia-Florida Contest in the American Revolution, 1776–1778*, 55–56.
51 Barrs, *East Florida in the American Revolution*, 10.
52 Searcy, *The Georgia-Florida Contest in the American Revolution, 1776–1778*, 56.
53 Smith, *The 14th Colony*, 10.
54 Smith, *The 14th Colony*, 10–12.
55 Raab, *Spain, Britain and the American Revolution in Florida, 1763–1783*, 109.
56 Smith, *The 14th Colony*, 10–12.
57 Searcy, *The Georgia-Florida Contest in the American Revolution, 1776–1778*, 57–59.
58 Bisset to Patrick Tonyn, September 1, 1776, Corse, *The Turnbull Papers*, 158.
59 Searcy, *The Georgia-Florida Contest in the American Revolution, 1776–1778*, 61–62.
60 Barrs, *East Florida in the American Revolution*, 10.
61 Smith, *The 14th Colony*, 19.
62 Barrs, *East Florida in the American Revolution*, 10.
63 Searcy, *The Georgia-Florida Contest in the American Revolution, 1776–1778*, 61–62, 65.
64 Governor Patrick Tonyn to Lord George Germain, October 30, 1776, Davies, *Documents of the American Revolution, 1770–1783* (Dublin: Irish University Press, 1976), 12: 243.
65 Searcy, *The Georgia-Florida Contest in the American Revolution, 1776–1778*, 66–78.

CHAPTER THREE. THE BATTLE OF THOMAS CREEK AND THE SECOND AMERICAN INVASION OF EAST FLORIDA

1 Searcy, *The Georgia-Florida Contest in the American Revolution, 1776–1778*, 80, 82, 84–85.
2 Barrs, *East Florida in the American Revolution*, 13.
3 Siebert, *Loyalists in East Florida, 1774–1785*, 1: 44–45.
4 Searcy, *The Georgia-Florida Contest in the American Revolution, 1776–1778*, 86.
5 Barrs, *East Florida in the American Revolution*, 13. An American force of 300 men encamped four miles away from the fort. This force refused to come to Winn's rescue after four Rangers shot at them (Searcy, 86).
6 Barrs, *East Florida in the American Revolution*, 16.

7 Searcy, *The Georgia-Florida Contest in the American Revolution, 1776–1778*, 86–87.

8 Siebert, *Loyalists in East Florida, 1774–1785*, 1: 45.

9 Barrs, *East Florida in the American Revolution*, 17. Of those 2,000 cattle, 1,800 crossed the St. Johns River. Tonyn sold them to dealers at 25 shillings a head (Siebert, 45). The beef was butchered and retailed in the public market for 3 pence a pound (Siebert, 45).

10 Searcy, *The Georgia-Florida Contest in the American Revolution, 1776–1778*, 88–89. For a review of Georgia's military strength at that time see Searcy, *The Georgia-Florida Contest in the American Revolution, 1776–1778*, 88–89.

11 George Washington to Brigadier General Robert Howe, March 17, 1777, *Founders Online*, National Archives, https://founders.archives.gov/documents/Washington/03-08-02-0633.

12 George Washington to Jonathan Bryan, March 17, 1777, *Founders Online*, National Archives, https://founders.archives.gov/documents/Washington/03-08-02-0631.

13 Smith, *The 14th Colony*, 20.

14 Searcy, *The Georgia-Florida Contest in the American Revolution, 1776–1778*, 89–90. Howe believed 7,000 to 8,000 men were needed merely to guard the Florida/Georgia border (Searcy, 89).

15 Barrs, *East Florida in the American Revolution*, 18.

16 These disputes were between Button Gwinnett and General Lachlan McIntosh over control of the 1777 expedition of East Florida. On many occasions Gwinnett tried assuming command of McIntosh's Continental troops. He arrogantly called a Council of War on April 14, 1777. McIntosh and his officers refused Gwinnett's power grab resulting in a standoff between the two men which eventually spread between the Continental Army officers and Georgia's Council of Safety. On April 19, the Council of Safety forced McIntosh to step down, naming Colonel Elbert the expedition leader. Angered, McIntosh requested a formal hearing with the Georgia Assembly to discuss what he believed to be Gwinnett's poor conduct and relations with the military. General McIntosh tried convincing the Assembly that Gwinnett's personal ambitions drove the East Florida expedition. Gwinnett, McIntosh asserted, refused to properly cooperate with the military and instead planned the expedition without their consultation. Gwinnett then had the audacity to claim that the military was noncooperative in the matter. McIntosh went on to call Gwinnett "a

Scoundrell and lying Rascal." In the end, the Assembly sided with Gwinnett, but the problem did not end there. Angered over what he believed to be public humiliation for calling him a scoundrel in public, Gwinnett challenged McIntosh to a duel. The two men met and shot each other in the thigh. Gwinnett did not survive his wounds (Wayne Lynch, "Button Gwinnett and Lachlan McIntosh Duel," *Journal of the American Revolution*, 24 September 2014, https://allthingsliberty.com/2014/09/button-gwinnett-and-the-mcintosh-duel/).

17 Searcy, *The Georgia-Florida Contest in the American Revolution, 1776–1778*, 90–93.

18 Barrs, *East Florida in the American Revolution*, 18–19.

19 Governor Patrick Tonyn to Lord George Germain, June 16, 1777, K. G. Davies, ed., *Documents of the American Revolution, 1770–1783 (Colonial Office Series)* (Dublin: Irish University Press, 1976), 14: 116–118.

20 Searcy, *The Georgia-Florida Contest in the American Revolution, 1776–1778*, 95.

21 Barrs, *East Florida in the American Revolution*, 19.

22 Searcy, *The Georgia-Florida Contest in the American Revolution, 1776–1778*, 93.

23 Barrs, *East Florida in the American Revolution*, 19.

24 Searcy, *The Georgia-Florida Contest in the American Revolution, 1776–1778*, 93.

25 Barrs, *East Florida in the American Revolution*, 19; Jim Piecuch, *Three Peoples, One King: Loyalists, Indians, and Slaves in the Revolutionary South, 1775–1782* (Columbia: University of South Carolina Press, 2008), 102.

26 Barrs, *East Florida in the American Revolution*, 19.

27 Schafer, "Chapter Thirteen," 213.

28 Barrs, *East Florida in the American Revolution*, 19.

29 Governor Patrick Tonyn to Lord George Germain, June 16, 1777, Davies, *Documents of the American Revolution, 1770–1783*, 14: 116–118.

30 Buker and Martin, "Governor Tonyn's Brown-Water Navy," 67.

31 Governor Patrick Tonyn to Lord George Germain, June 16, 1777, Davies, *Documents of the American Revolution, 1770–1783*, 14: 116–118.

32 Buker and Martin, "Governor Tonyn's Brown-Water Navy," 67.

33 Searcy, *The Georgia-Florida Contest in the American Revolution, 1776–1778*, 96.

34 Barrs, *East Florida in the American Revolution*, 19–20.

35 Searcy, *The Georgia-Florida Contest in the American Revolution, 1776–1778*, 96, 100, 110, 113.
36 Mowat, *East Florida as a British Province*, 71–72.
37 Corse, *Dr. Andrew Turnbull and The New Smyrna Colony of Florida*, 19.
38 Mowat, *East Florida as a British Province*, 72.
39 Schafer, "Chapter Nine," 129. For more on the Minorcans see Patricia C. Griffin's *Mullet on the Beach: The Minorcans of Florida, 1768–1788* (Gainesville: University Press of Florida, 1991).
40 Mowat, *East Florida as a British Province*, 72.
41 Hoffman, *Florida's Frontiers*, 219–220.
42 Corse, *Dr. Andrew Turnbull and The New Smyrna Colony of Florida*, 24–28.
43 Mowat, *East Florida as a British Province*, 72.
44 VanDoren, *Travels of William Bartram*, 134.
45 VanDoren, *Travels of William Bartram*, 134.
46 Wilbur Henry Siebert, "Slavery and White Servitude in East Florida, 1726–1776," *The Florida Historical Quarterly* 10, no. 1 (July 1931): 18.
47 Panagopoulos, *New Smyrna*, 58, 87.
48 Beeson Jr., *Fromajadas and Indigo*, 63, 82–83.
49 Panagopoulos, *New Smyrna*, 59, 83, 85–86, 91–92.
50 Patrick Tonyn to George Germain, May 8, 1777, Corse, *The Turnbull Papers*, 211.
51 Beeson Jr., *Fromajadas and Indigo*, 82.
52 Piecuch, "Patrick Tonyn: Britain's Most Effective Revolutionary-Era Royal Governor."
53 Patrick Tonyn to George Germain, August 21, 1776.
54 Patrick Tonyn to Augustine Prevost, December 24, 1777, *The On-Line Institute for Advanced Loyalist Studies*, transcribed by Todd Braisted, http://www.royalprovincial.com/military/facts/ofrlet8.htm.
55 Patrick Tonyn to George Germain, August 21, 1776.
56 Patrick Tonyn to George Germain, May 8, 1777, Corse, *The Turnbull Papers*, 211.
57 Andrew Turnbull Jr. to Arthur Gordon, September 1, 1776, Corse, *The Turnbull Papers*, 157.
58 Andrew Turnbull Jr. to Arthur Gordon, September 1, 1776, Corse, *The Turnbull Papers*, 157; Corse, *Dr. Andrew Turnbull and The New Smyrna Colony of Florida*, 103.
59 Patrick Tonyn to George Germain, September 8, 1776, Corse, *The Turnbull Papers*, 159.

60 Bisset to Patrick Tonyn, September 1, 1776, Corse, *The Turnbull Papers*, 158.

61 Bisset to Patrick Tonyn, September 1, 1776, Corse, *The Turnbull Papers*, 158.

62 Corse, *Dr. Andrew Turnbull and The New Smyrna Colony of Florida*, 157.

63 Patrick Tonyn to George Germain, May 8, 1777, Corse, *The Turnbull Papers*, 211–212.

64 While some Minorcans attempted to negotiate with Tonyn, others escaped and joined the crews of rebel privateers operating around New Smyrna (Wright Jr., 57).

65 Corse, *Dr. Andrew Turnbull and The New Smyrna Colony of Florida*, 157–159, 163.

66 Patrick Tonyn to George Germain, July 26, 1777, Corse, *The Turnbull Papers*, 220.

67 Corse, *Dr. Andrew Turnbull and The New Smyrna Colony of Florida*, 164–165.

68 Schafer, "Chapter Twelve," 199.

69 Schafer, "Chapter Thirteen," 219.

70 Andrew Turnbull to Earl of Shelburne, November 10, 1777, Corse, *The Turnbull Papers*, 221.

71 Corse, *Dr. Andrew Turnbull and The New Smyrna Colony of Florida*, 170.

72 Andrew Turnbull to Earl of Shelburne, November 10, 1777, Corse, *The Turnbull Papers*, 221.

73 Beeson Jr., *Fromajadas and Indigo*, 83.

74 Corse, *Dr. Andrew Turnbull and The New Smyrna Colony of Florida*, 186, 192–194.

75 Patrick Tonyn to Thomas Townshend (Lord Sydney), April 4, 1785, Corse, *The Turnbull Papers*, 359–360.

76 Beeson Jr., *Fromajadas and Indigo*, 83.

CHAPTER FOUR. THE BATTLE OF ALLIGATOR CREEK BRIDGE AND THE THIRD AMERICAN INVASION OF EAST FLORIDA

1 The Americans were not alone in desiring East Florida's conquest. The Spanish, too, eyed East Florida. Early in 1778, Captain General of Cuba, Don Diego Joseph Navarro, created an invasion plan for St. Augustine to be put into effect once Spain declared war on Great Britain. Navarro's invasion force would launch from Havana. Spanish

officials rejected Navarro's plan (Light T. Cummins, "Luciano de Herrera and Spanish Espionage in British St. Augustine," *El Escribano: The St. Augustine Journal of History* 16 (1979): 53–54.

2 Worthington Chauncey Ford, ed., *Journals of the Continental Congress, 1774–1789* (Washington: Government Printing Press, 1908), 10: 163.

3 Searcy, *The Georgia-Florida Contest in the American Revolution, 1776–1778*, 126–128.

4 Searcy, *The Georgia-Florida Contest in the American Revolution, 1776–1778*, 129–130. Historians disagree on exactly when this battle took place. Edward Cashin claims the battle occurred on March 12, 1778, while Martha Searcy claims it occurred on March 13.

5 Cashin, *The King's Ranger*, 74.

6 Searcy, *The Georgia-Florida Contest in the American Revolution, 1776–1778*, 131.

7 Cashin, *The King's Ranger*, 75.

8 Gary D. Olson, "Thomas Brown, the East Florida Rangers, and the Defense of East Florida." In *Eighteenth-Century Florida and the Revolutionary South*, edited by Samuel Proctor (Gainesville: University Presses of Florida, 1978), 24.

9 For more on Britain's southern strategy see Jim Piecuch's *Three Peoples, One King: Loyalists, Indians, and Slaves in the Revolutionary South, 1775–1782* (Columbia: University of South Carolina Press, 2008).

10 Barrs, *East Florida in the American Revolution*, 23.

11 Smith, *The 14th Colony*, 26.

12 Barrs, *East Florida in the American Revolution*, 23, 25.

13 Searcy, *The Georgia-Florida Contest in the American Revolution, 1776–1778*, 134–135.

14 Barrs, *East Florida in the American Revolution*, 23.

15 Searcy, *The Georgia-Florida Contest in the American Revolution, 1776–1778*, 136.

16 For more on this see Gary D. Olson's "Thomas Brown, the East Florida Rangers, and the Defense of East Florida." In *Eighteenth-Century Florida and the Revolutionary South*, edited by Samuel Proctor (Gainesville: University Presses of Florida, 1978), 15–28.

17 Buker and Martin, "Governor Tonyn's Brown-Water Navy," 69–70.

18 Buker and Martin, "Governor Tonyn's Brown-Water Navy," 69–70.

19 Searcy, *The Georgia-Florida Contest in the American Revolution, 1776–1778*, 138–139.

20 Siebert, *Loyalists in East Florida, 1774–1785*, 1: 56.

21 Searcy, *The Georgia-Florida Contest in the American Revolution, 1776–1778*, 140–142.
22 Barrs, *East Florida in the American Revolution*, 27.
23 Gold, *History of Duval County Including Early History of East Florida*, 58.
24 Searcy, *The Georgia-Florida Contest in the American Revolution, 1776–1778*, 142–143.
25 Cashin, *The King's Ranger*, 77–78.
26 Searcy, *The Georgia-Florida Contest in the American Revolution, 1776–1778*, 143; Cashin, *The King's Ranger*, 77–78.
27 Searcy, *The Georgia-Florida Contest in the American Revolution, 1776–1778*, 143.
28 Barrs, *East Florida in the American Revolution*, 27.
29 Searcy, *The Georgia-Florida Contest in the American Revolution, 1776–1778*, 144.
30 Barrs, *East Florida in the American Revolution*, 27; Searcy, *The Georgia-Florida Contest in the American Revolution, 1776–1778*, 143.
31 Barrs, *East Florida in the American Revolution*, 27.
32 Cashin, *The King's Ranger*, 78; Barrs, *East Florida in the American Revolution*, 27.
33 Wright Jr., *Florida in the American Revolution*, 56.
34 Barrs, *East Florida in the American Revolution*, 27.
35 Cashin, *The King's Ranger*, 78.
36 Barrs, *East Florida in the American Revolution*, 27.
37 Barrs, *East Florida in the American Revolution*, 27–28.
38 Searcy, *The Georgia-Florida Contest in the American Revolution, 1776–1778*, 145.
39 Barrs, *East Florida in the American Revolution*, 28.
40 Searcy, *The Georgia-Florida Contest in the American Revolution, 1776–1778*, 142–143, 145–147.
41 Siebert, *Loyalists in East Florida, 1774–1785*, I: 59.
42 Searcy, *The Georgia-Florida Contest in the American Revolution, 1776–1778*, 152.
43 Wright Jr., *Florida in the American Revolution*, 57–58.
44 Hoffman, *Florida's Frontiers*, 227.
45 Searcy, *The Georgia-Florida Contest in the American Revolution, 1776–1778*, 154–155.
46 Siebert, *Loyalists in East Florida, 1774–1785*, I: 60.
47 Panagopoulos, *New Smyrna*, 165; Siebert, *Loyalists in East Florida, 1774–1785*, I: 60.

48 Edgar Legare Pennington, "East Florida in the American Revolution, 1775–1778," *The Florida Historical Quarterly* 9, no. 1 (July 1930): 46.
49 Wright Jr., *Florida in the American Revolution*, 82–83.
50 Searcy, *The Georgia-Florida Contest in the American Revolution, 1776–1778*, 155–156; Wright Jr., *Florida in the American Revolution*, 58.
51 Piecuch, *Three Peoples, One King*, 126–127.
52 Searcy, *The Georgia-Florida Contest in the American Revolution, 1776–1778*, 159.
53 Piecuch, *Three Peoples, One King*, 126–127.
54 Searcy, *The Georgia-Florida Contest in the American Revolution, 1776–1778*, 160.
55 Searcy, *The Georgia-Florida Contest in the American Revolution, 1776–1778*, 157.
56 Smith, *The 14th Colony*, 30.
57 Searcy, *The Georgia-Florida Contest in the American Revolution, 1776–1778*, 157.
58 Smith, *The 14th Colony*, 30.
59 Searcy, *The Georgia-Florida Contest in the American Revolution, 1776–1778*, 161–162.
60 Wayne Lynch, "James Screven—Ambushed!" *Journal of the American Revolution*, 13 March 2014, https://allthingsliberty.com/2014/03/james-screven-ambushed/.
61 Searcy, *The Georgia-Florida Contest in the American Revolution, 1776–1778*, 162–163.
62 Barrs, *East Florida in the American Revolution*, 30.
63 Searcy, *The Georgia-Florida Contest in the American Revolution, 1776–1778*, 163.
64 Searcy, *The Georgia-Florida Contest in the American Revolution, 1776–1778*, 164.
65 Barrs, *East Florida in the American Revolution*, 30.
66 Siebert, *Loyalists in East Florida, 1774–1785*, 1: 73.
67 Searcy, *The Georgia-Florida Contest in the American Revolution, 1776–1778*, 167.
68 Barrs, *East Florida in the American Revolution*, 30–31.
69 Searcy, *The Georgia-Florida Contest in the American Revolution, 1776–1778*, 167.
70 Piecuch, *Three Peoples, One King*, 132–133.
71 Searcy, *The Georgia-Florida Contest in the American Revolution, 1776–1778*, 168.
72 Barrs, *East Florida in the American Revolution*, 31.

73 Schafer, "Chapter Twelve," 206.
74 Searcy, *The Georgia-Florida Contest in the American Revolution, 1776–1778*, 164–165.
75 Barrs, *East Florida in the American Revolution*, 31.
76 Schafer, "Chapter Twelve," 206.
77 Lord George Germain to Alexander Cameron and Lieutenant Colonel Thomas Brown, June 25, 1779, K. G. Davies, ed., *Documents of the American Revolution, 1770–1783 (Colonial Office Series)* (Dublin: Irish University Press, 1977), 17: 154–155.
78 Wright Jr., *Florida in the American Revolution*, 58, 74–75.

CHAPTER FIVE. BRITISH EAST FLORIDA'S FINAL YEARS

1 Franklin and Lafayette's List of Prints to Illustrate British Cruelties, [c. May 1779], *Founders Online*, National Archives, https://founders.archives.gov/documents/Franklin/01–29-02–0477.
2 Smith, *The 14th Colony*, 31.
3 Major General Benjamin Lincoln to George Washington, January 28–29, 1780, *Founders Online*, National Archives, https://founders.archives.gov/documents/Washington/03–24-02–0237.
4 Smith, *The 14th Colony*, 31.
5 Mowat, *East Florida as a British Province*, 125.
6 Hoffman, *Florida's Frontiers*, 229.
7 Wright Jr., *Florida in the American Revolution*, 67, 71, 82.
8 Hoffman, *Florida's Frontiers*, 227; Governor Patrick Tonyn to Lord George Germain, January 27, 1780, K. G. Davies, *Documents of the American Revolution, 1770–1783 (Colonial Office Series)* (Dublin: Irish University Press, 1979), 20: 46–47.
9 For more on the Hessians in East Florida see George Kotlik's "The Hessians in East Florida, 1781," in *The Hessians: Journal of the Johannes Schwalm Historical Association* (2020): 76–80. According to Kotlik, Hessians from the von Knoblauch Regiment were stationed in East Florida in 1781. What's more, Germans from the 4th Battalion of the 60th Regiment of Foot served in East Florida. Germans from the 60th Regiment were recruited in the outskirts of Hanover (Lewis Butler, *The Annals of the King's Royal Rifle Corps: "The Royal Americans"* (Naval & Military Press), 1: 208). By 1778, 400 German soldiers from the 60th Regiment guarded St. Augustine (Memorial and Particulars relative to Ft. St. Augustine with a Plan of attack and Military Operations

necessary for the Reduction of that Place, by Marquis de Bretigny, August 26, 1778. U.S. Continental Congress. Papers of the Continental Congress, 1774–89. National Archives and Records Service. Microfilm. Florida State University Library).

10 Wright Jr., *Florida in the American Revolution*, 95.

11 Thomas E. Chavez, *Spain and the Independence of the United States: An Intrinsic Gift* (Albuquerque: University of New Mexico Press, 2002), 204.

12 Chavez, *Spain and the Independence of the United States*, 134.

13 Wright Jr., *Florida in the American Revolution*, 67–68.

14 Wright Jr., *Florida in the American Revolution*, 67. The Spaniards delivered holy oil to the Minorcan Catholics. The 1763 Treaty of Paris guaranteed freedom of religion to all inhabitants of East Florida, making such an arrangement possible (Michael V. Gannan, "Mitres and Flags: Colonial Religion in the British and Second Spanish Periods," In *Eighteenth-Century Florida: The Impact of the American Revolution*, edited by Samuel Proctor (Gainesville: University Presses of Florida, 1978), 83–84).

15 Schafer, "Chapter Thirteen," 221–222; For more on Luciano de Herrera and Spanish spying in East Florida see Light T. Cummins's "Luciano de Herrera and Spanish Espionage in British St. Augustine," *El Escribano: The St. Augustine Journal of History* 16 (1979): 43–57 and Chavez's *Spain and the Independence of the United States*, 122.

16 Schafer, "Chapter Thirteen," 222. Luciano de Herrera returned to East Florida during the Second Spanish Period and was appointed East Florida's Chief Overseer of Works, his reward for spying on the British during the American Revolution. Luciano also became an intermediary between the Spanish government and the Seminole and Creek Indians (Raab, 181; Daniel L. Schafer, "Chapter Fifteen: 'realizing something out of the Wreck,'" *El Escribano: The St. Augustine Journal of History: St. Augustine's British Years 1763–1784* 38 (2001): 266).

17 For more on smallpox during the American Revolutionary War see Elizabeth A. Fenn's *Pox Americana: The Great Smallpox Epidemic of 1775–1782* (New York: Hill & Wang, 2002).

18 Governor Patrick Tonyn to Lord George Germain, December 9, 1780, K. G. Davies, *Documents of the American Revolution, 1770–1783*, 18: 252–253.

19 Mowat, *East Florida as a British Province*, 127. J. Leitch Wright Jr. believes that had the British not captured Savannah in 1778, the French

fleet under the Comte d'Estaing would have attacked St. Augustine instead (Wright Jr., 82).

20 Wright Jr., *Florida in the American Revolution*, 95.

21 Mowat, *East Florida as a British Province*, 127–128, 130–132.

22 Governor Patrick Tonyn to Lord George Germain, November 30, 1781, Davies, *Documents of the American Revolution, 1770–1783*, 20: 266–267.

23 Mowat, *East Florida as a British Province*, 130–131.

24 Siebert, *Loyalists in East Florida, 1774–1785*, 1: 98–99.

25 Gold, *History of Duval County Including Early History of East Florida*, 58–59.

26 Mowat, *East Florida as a British Province*, 128–129, 131–134.

27 Andrew Jackson O'Shaughnessy, *The Men Who Lost America: British Leadership, the American Revolution, and the Fate of the Empire* (New Haven: Yale University Press, 2013), 41–43.

28 Nester, *The Frontier War for American Independence*, 321.

29 Mowat, *East Florida as a British Province*, 140–141.

30 Raab, *Spain, Britain and the American Revolution in Florida, 1763–1783*, 164.

31 Mowat, *East Florida as a British Province*, 137, 141.

32 Carole Watterson Troxler, "Loyalist Refugees and the British Evacuation of East Florida, 1783–1785," *The Florida Historical Quarterly* 60, no. 1 (July 1981): 1–3.

33 *East Florida Gazette*, Volume I Number 16, May 10 to May 17, 1783.

34 Mowat, *East Florida as a British Province*, 142, 144; Raab, *Spain, Britain and the American Revolution in Florida, 1763–1783*, 173.

35 Lord North to Governor Patrick Tonyn, December 4, 1783, Davies, *Documents of the American Revolution, 1770–1783*, 21: 251–252.

36 To get a general sense of how East Florida residents felt about their forced evacuation see M. Tattnall to John Street, May 30, 1783, Davies, *Documents of the American Revolution, 1770–1783*, 21: 173–175.

37 M. Tattnall to John Street, May 30, 1783, Davies, *Documents of the American Revolution, 1770–1783*, 21: 173.

38 M. Tattnall to John Street, May 30, 1783, Davies, *Documents of the American Revolution, 1770–1783*, 21: 173–174.

39 M. Tattnall to John Street, May 30, 1783, Davies, *Documents of the American Revolution, 1770–1783*, 21: 175.

40 *East Florida Gazette*, Volume I Number 5, February 22 to March 1, 1783.

41 Hoffman, *Florida's Frontiers*, 231.
42 Mowat, *East Florida as a British Province*, 142–143.
43 Joseph B. Lockey, "The Florida Banditti, 1783," *The Florida Historical Quarterly* 24, no. 2 (October 1945): 87–88.
44 Troxler, "Loyalist Refugees and the British Evacuation of East Florida, 1783–1785," 6. William Cunningham, otherwise known as "Bloody Bill Cunningham," was a member of McGirtt's gang (Troxler, 16). For more on Daniel McGirtt and his exploits see Wayne Lynch's "Daniel McGirth, Banditti on the Southern Frontier," *Journal of the American Revolution*, August 23, 2016, https://allthingsliberty.com/2016/08/daniel-mcgirth-banditti-southern-frontier/.
45 Mowat, *East Florida as a British Province*, 143.
46 Troxler, "Loyalist Refugees and the British Evacuation of East Florida, 1783–1785," 6.
47 Lockey, "The Florida Banditti, 1783," 88.
48 Troxler, "Loyalist Refugees and the British Evacuation of East Florida, 1783–1785," 16.
49 Troxler, "Loyalist Refugees and the British Evacuation of East Florida, 1783–1785," 9–12.
50 Raab, *Spain, Britain and the American Revolution in Florida, 1763–1783*, 174.
51 Hoffman, *Florida's Frontiers*, 231.
52 Wright Jr., *Florida in the American Revolution*, 137.
53 Wright Jr., *Florida in the American Revolution*, 133–134.
54 Hoffman, *Florida's Frontiers*, 232.
55 Johann David Schoepf, *Travels in the Confederation, 1783–1784*, ed. Alfred J. Morrison (Philadelphia: William J. Campbell, 1911), 2: 240.
56 Nester, *The Frontier War for American Independence*, 335-336.
57 Wright Jr., *Florida in the American Revolution*, 134.
58 Raab, *Spain, Britain and the American Revolution in Florida, 1763–1783*, 169.
59 Siebert, *Loyalists in East Florida, 1774–1785*, 1: 155.
60 Mowat, *East Florida as a British Province*, 145; Troxler, "Loyalist Refugees and the British Evacuation of East Florida, 1783–1785," 14–15.
61 Governor Patrick Tonyn to Thomas Townshend, May 15, 1783, Davies, *Documents of the American Revolution, 1770–1783*, 21: 166–169.
62 Wright Jr., *Florida in the American Revolution*, 133.
63 Siebert, *Loyalists in East Florida, 1774–1785*, 1: 134–136.
64 A few members of the St. Augustine Historical Society believe that

most editions of the *East Florida Gazette* were accidentally dumped in the water during the chaotic British evacuation. Some editions may still survive in private collections or are lost in someone's attic.

65 Mowat, *East Florida as a British Province*, 139.

66 Observations of Grand Jury of East Florida, December 20, 1775, K. G. Davies, ed., *Documents of the American Revolution, 1770–1783 (Colonial Office Series)* (Dublin: Irish University Press, 1973), 11: 215.

67 Wright Jr., *Florida in the American Revolution*, 148.

68 Mowat, *East Florida as a British Province*, 138–139.

69 David D. Mays, "Theatre Can't Get Here from There: A Brief Production History of Florida's First Play," in *Eighteenth-Century Florida: Life on the Frontier*, edited by Samuel Proctor (Gainesville: University Presses of Florida, 1976), 97–98.

70 Mowat, *East Florida as a British Province*, 138–139.

71 Mays, "Theatre Can't Get Here from There: A Brief Production History of Florida's First Play," 97.

72 Mays, "Theatre Can't Get Here from There: A Brief Production History of Florida's First Play," 99.

73 Wright Jr., *Florida in the American Revolution*, 98.

74 For more on the British invasion of the Bahamas in 1783 see Catherine S. Crary's *The Price of Loyalty: Tory Writings from the Revolutionary Era* (New York: McGraw-Hill Book Company, 1973); Michael Craton's *A History of the Bahamas* (London: Collins, 1963); Michael Craton and Gail Saunders' *Islanders in the Stream: A History of the Bahamian People, Volume I: From Aboriginal Times to the End of Slavery* (Athens, University of Georgia Press, 1992); David F. Marley's *Wars of the Americas: A Chronology of Armed Conflict in the New World, 1492 to the Present* (Denver: ABC-CLIO, 1998); Mowat's *East Florida as a British Province, 1763–1784*; Siebert's *Loyalists in East Florida, 1774–1785*; Wilbur Henry Siebert's *The Legacy of the American Revolution to the British West Indies and Bahamas: A Chapter out of the History of the American Loyalists* (Boston: Gregg Press, 1972); *East Florida Gazette*, Volume I Number 14, April 26 to May 3, 1783; and James A. Lewis's *The Final Campaign of the American Revolution: Rise and Fall of the Spanish Bahamas* (Columbia: University of South Carolina Press, 1991).

75 Schafer, "Chapter Fourteen," 245.

76 Craton, *A History of the Bahamas*, 160.

77 Schafer, "Chapter Fourteen: The Fate of East Florida," 245.

78 Craton and Saunders, *Islanders in the Stream*, 1: 169.

79 Siebert, *Loyalists in East Florida, 1774–1785*, 1: 145; Crary, *The Price of Loyalty*, 355.
80 Governor Patrick Tonyn to Thomas Townshend, May 15, 1783, Davies, *Documents of the American Revolution, 1770–1783*, 21: 169.
81 *East Florida Gazette*, Volume I Number 14, April 26 to May 3, 1783. Crary indicates the expedition set out with sixty-five men, Siebert also says sixty-five men. The *East Florida Gazette* says forty to fifty.
82 Marley, *Wars of the Americas*, 346.
83 Craton and Saunders, *Islanders in the Stream*, 1: 170.
84 *East Florida Gazette*, Volume I Number 14, April 26 to May 3, 1783.
85 Siebert, *Loyalists in East Florida, 1774–1785*, 1: 147.
86 Crary, *The Price of Loyalty*, 355.
87 Craton, *A History of the Bahamas*, 161.
88 Craton and Saunders, *Islanders in the Stream*, 1: 171.
89 Mowat, *East Florida as a British Province*, 145.
90 Wright Jr., *Florida in the American Revolution*, 135.
91 Hoffman, *Florida's Frontiers*, 232.
92 Mowat, *East Florida as a British Province*, 145.
93 Wright Jr., *Florida in the American Revolution*, 135–136.
94 Schafer, "Chapter Fifteen," 254.
95 Mowat, *East Florida as a British Province*, 146.
96 Raab, *Spain, Britain and the American Revolution in Florida, 1763–1783*, 175.
97 Mowat, *East Florida as a British Province*, 146.
98 Hoffman, *Florida's Frontiers*, 234; Troxler, "Loyalist Refugees and the British Evacuation of East Florida, 1783–1785," 15.
99 Schafer, "Chapter Fifteen," 263.
100 "Appendix A: Historic Context and References," *The Historic Properties Resurvey, City of Fernandina Beach, Nassau County, Florida* (Bland and Associates Inc., 2007), 5; Schafer, "Chapter Fifteen," 263.
101 Troxler, "Loyalist Refugees and the British Evacuation of East Florida, 1783–1785," 23–24.
102 Raab, *Spain, Britain and the American Revolution in Florida, 1763–1783*, 170.
103 Troxler, "Loyalist Refugees and the British Evacuation of East Florida, 1783–1785," 26. Tonyn initially departed East Florida on September 11, 1785, but his ship, the *Cyrus*, was damaged from rotten wood (Troxler, 25–26). Two ships from Nassau had to come to Tonyn's rescue (Troxler, 25–26).

104 Mowat, *East Florida as a British Province*, 147; Siebert, *Loyalists in East Florida, 1774–1785*, 1: 181–210. See graph in Siebert, *Loyalists in East Florida, 1774–1785*, 1: 208. According to Dr. Roger Smith, after the British evacuated, "3,589 African Americans were sent to work on Caribbean sugar plantations; 2,561 were returned to their United States owners; 200 applied for Spanish citizenship; 155 went to Nova Scotia; and 35 to Deptford, England" (Smith, *Hope of Freedom*, 32).

105 Wright Jr., *Florida in the American Revolution*, 139, 142–143, 145, 148–149.

106 Wright Jr., *Florida in the American Revolution*, 140.

107 Raab, *Spain, Britain and the American Revolution in Florida, 1763–1783*, 178.

108 Mowat, *East Florida as a British Province*, 147–148.

109 Wright Jr., *Florida in the American Revolution*, 141.

110 Raab, *Spain, Britain and the American Revolution in Florida, 1763–1783*, 180–181.

111 Raab, *Spain, Britain and the American Revolution in Florida, 1763–1783*, 176.

112 Mowat, *East Florida as a British Province*, 149; Wright Jr., *Florida in the American Revolution*, 139; Raab, *Spain, Britain and the American Revolution in Florida, 1763–1783*, 97.

113 For more on loyalist reintegration see Rebecca Brannon's *From Revolution to Reunion: The Reintegration of the South Carolina Loyalists* (Columbia: University of South Carolina Press, 2016).

114 Wright Jr., *Florida in the American Revolution*, 128, 131, 138–139, 151–152.

115 Raab, *Spain, Britain and the American Revolution in Florida, 1763–1783*, 143.

116 Mowat, *East Florida as a British Province*, 149.

CONCLUSION

1 Wright Jr., *Florida in the American Revolution*, 149.

2 Kathleen DuVal, *Independence Lost: Lives on the Edge of the American Revolution* (New York: Random House, 2015), xxiv, 340–351.

3 Wright Jr., *Florida in the American Revolution*, 146.

4 Siebert, *Loyalists in East Florida, 1774–1785*, 1: 178.

5 Wright Jr., *Florida in the American Revolution*, 147.

6 Siebert, *Loyalists in East Florida, 1774–1785*, 1: 178.

7 DuVal, *Independence Lost*, 328; Tanner, "Pipesmoke and Muskets," 35.

8 David Narrett, *Adventurism and Empire: The Struggle for Mastery in the Louisiana-Florida Borderlands, 1762–1803* (Chapel Hill: University of North Carolina Press, 2015), 212.
9 Siebert, *Loyalists in East Florida, 1774–1785*, 1: 178.
10 Narrett, *Adventurism and Empire*, 213.
11 Siebert, *Loyalists in East Florida, 1774–1785*, 1: 178–179.
12 Narrett, *Adventurism and Empire*, 213, 215–217, 218. This flag had a cross and the emblem of a sun with facial features.
13 Siebert, *Loyalists in East Florida, 1774–1785*, 1: 179.
14 Narrett, *Adventurism and Empire*, 260.
15 Siebert, *Loyalists in East Florida, 1774–1785*, 1: 179.
16 Narrett, *Adventurism and Empire*, 260–261.
17 Siebert, *Loyalists in East Florida, 1774–1785*, 1: 179.
18 Wright Jr., *Florida in the American Revolution*, 146, 147.
19 Mowat, *East Florida as a British Province*, 148.

Bibliography

PRIMARY SOURCES

Collections of the Georgia Historical Society. Volume V. Part 1. Savannah: Braid & Hutton, Printers & Binders, 1901.

Corse, Carita Doggett, ed. *The Turnbull Papers*. Jacksonville, 1940.

Davies, K. G., ed. *Documents of the American Revolution, 1770–1783 (Colonial Office Series)*. 21 Volumes. Dublin: Irish University Press, 1972–1981.

East Florida Gazette, Volume I Number 5, February 22 to March 1, 1783.

East Florida Gazette, Volume I Number 14, April 26 to May 3, 1783.

East Florida Gazette, Volume I Number 16, May 10 to May 17, 1783.

Ford, Worthington Chauncey, ed. *Journals of the Continental Congress, 1774–1789*. Volumes 1, 2, 4, 10. Washington: Government Printing Press, 1904–08.

Franklin and Lafayette's List of Prints to Illustrate British Cruelties, [c. May 1779]. *Founders Online*. National Archives. https://founders.archives.gov/documents/Franklin/01–29-02–0477.

Lincoln, Major General Benjamin to George Washington, 28–29 January 1780. *Founders Online*. National Archives. https://founders.archives.gov/documents/Washington/03–24-02–0237.

"Memorial and Particulars relative to Ft. St. Augustine with a Plan of attack and Military Operations necessary for the Reduction of that Place," by Marquis de Bretigny, August 26, 1778. U. S. Continental Congress. Papers of the Continental Congress, 1774–89. National Archives and Records Service. Microfilm. Florida State University Library.

Romans, Bernard. *A Concise Natural History of East and West Florida*. New York: R. Aitken, 1776.

Schoepf, Johann David. *Travels in the Confederation, 1783–1784*. Edited by Alfred J. Morrison. Vol. II. Philadelphia: William J. Campbell, 1911.

"Sketch of Propositions for a Peace" [after 26 September 1776 and before 25 October 1776]. *Founders Online*. National Archives. https://founders.archives.gov/documents/Franklin/01–22-02–0372.

Tonyn, Patrick to General Henry Clinton, April 15, 1776. *The On-Line Insti-*

tute for Advanced Loyalist Studies. Transcribed by Todd Braisted. http://www.royalprovincial.com/military/rhist/eastfr/easttonı.htm.

Tonyn, Patrick to Lord George Germain, August 21, 1776. *The On-Line Institute for Advanced Loyalist Studies*. Transcribed by Todd Braisted. http://www.royalprovincial.com/military/rhist/eastflmil/eflmillet1.htm.

Tonyn, Patrick to Augustine Prevost, December 24, 1777. *The On-Line Institute for Advanced Loyalist Studies*. Transcribed by Todd Braisted. http://www.royalprovincial.com/military/facts/ofrlet8.htm.

VanDoren, Mark, ed. *Travels of William Bartram*. New York: Dover Publications, 1955.

Washington, George to Brigadier General Robert Howe, 17 March 1777. *Founders Online*. National Archives. https://founders.archives.gov/documents/Washington/03-08-02-0633.

ARTICLES AND BOOKS

"Appendix A: Historic Context and References." *The Historic Properties Resurvey, City of Fernandina Beach, Nassau County, Florida*. Bland and Associates Inc., 2007.

Arana, Luis Rafael. "British Regiments in St. Augustine, 1763–1784." *El Escribano: The St. Augustine Journal of History: Defenses and Defenders at St. Augustine* 36 (1999): 114–118.

Arana, Luis Rafael. "Construction at Castillo de San Marcos." *El Escribano: The St. Augustine Journal of History: Defenses and Defenders at St. Augustine* 36 (1999): 119–126.

Arana, Luis Rafael. "Don Manuel de Cendoya and Castillo de San Marcos, 1669–1673." *El Escribano: The St. Augustine Journal of History: Defenses and Defenders at St. Augustine* 36 (1999): 29–36.

Arana, Luis Rafael. "Governor Cendoya's Negotiations in Mexico for a Stone Fort in St. Augustine." *El Escribano: The St. Augustine Journal of History: Defenses and Defenders at St. Augustine* 36 (1999): 22–28.

Arana, Luis Rafael. "The Basis of a Permanent Fortification." *El Escribano: The St. Augustine Journal of History: Defenses and Defenders at St. Augustine* 36 (1999): 3–10.

Arana, Luis Rafael. "The Cubo Line, 1704–1909." *El Escribano: The St. Augustine Journal of History: Defenses and Defenders at St. Augustine* 36 (1999): 187–210.

Bailyn, Bernard. *Voyagers to the West: A Passage in the Peopling of America on the Eve of the Revolution*. New York: Alfred A. Knopf, 1986.

Barrs, Burton. *East Florida in the American Revolution*. Jacksonville: The Cooper Press, 1949.

Baugh, Daniel. *The Global Seven Years' War 1754–1763*. New York: Routledge, 2014.

Beeson Jr., Kenneth H. *Fromajadas and Indigo: The Minorcan Colony in Florida*. Charleston: The History Press, 2006.

Boyd, Mark F. "A Map of the Road from Pensacola to St. Augustine, 1778." *The Florida Historical Quarterly* 17, no. 1 (July 1938): 15–23.

Buker, George E., and Richard Apley Martin. "Governor Tonyn's Brown-Water Navy: East Florida During the American Revolution, 1775–1778." *The Florida Historical Quarterly* 58, no. 1 (July 1979): 58–71.

Butler, Lewis. *The Annals of the King's Royal Rifle Corps*. Vol. 1, *"The Royal Americans"* Naval & Military Press.

Calloway, Colin G. *The Scratch of a Pen: 1763 and the Transformation of North America*. New York: Oxford University Press, 2006.

Carrington, Selwyn H. H. "The American Revolution and the British West Indies' Economy." *The Journal of Interdisciplinary History* 17, no. 4 (Spring 1987): 823–850.

Cashin, Edward J. *Governor Henry Ellis and the Transformation of British North America*. Athens: The University of Georgia Press, 1994.

Cashin, Edward J. *The King's Ranger: Thomas Brown and the American Revolution on the Southern Frontier*. Athens: The University of Georgia Press, 1989.

Chavez, Thomas E. *Spain and the Independence of the United States: An Intrinsic Gift*. Albuquerque: University of New Mexico Press, 2002.

Chesnutt, David R. "South Carolina's Impact upon East Florida, 1763–1776." In *Eighteenth-Century Florida and the Revolutionary South*, edited by Samuel Proctor, 5–14. Gainesville: The University Presses of Florida, 1978.

Coker, William S. "Entrepreneurs in the British and Spanish Floridas, 1775–1821." In *Eighteenth-Century Florida and the Caribbean*, edited by Samuel Proctor, 15–39. Gainesville: The University Presses of Florida, 1976.

Corse, Carita Doggett and Grant, James. "Denys Rolle and Rollestown, a Pioneer for Utopia." *The Florida Historical Society Quarterly* 7, no. 2 (October 1928): 115–134.

Corse, Carita Doggett. *Dr. Andrew Turnbull and The New Smyrna Colony of Florida*. Florida: The Drew Press, 1919.

Crary, Catherine S. *The Price of Loyalty: Tory Writings from the Revolutionary Era*. New York: McGraw-Hill Book Company, 1973.

Craton, Michael. *A History of the Bahamas*. London: Collins, 1963.

Craton, Michael and Gail Saunders. *Islanders in the Stream: A History of the Bahamian People, Volume I: From Aboriginal Times to the End of Slavery*. Athens: The University of Georgia Press, 1992.

Cummins, Light T. "Luciano de Herrera and Spanish Espionage in British St. Augustine." *El Escribano: The St. Augustine Journal of History* 16 (1979): 43–57.

De Vorsey Jr., Louis. "De Brahm's East Florida on the Eve of Revolution: The Materials for Its Re-creation." In *Eighteenth-Century Florida and Its Borderlands*, edited by Samuel Proctor, 78–96. Gainesville: The University Presses of Florida, 1975.

Dickerson, Oliver Morton. *American Colonial Government 1696–1765: A study of the British Board of Trade in its relation to the American Colonies, Political, Industrial, Administrative.* Cleveland: The Arthur H. Clark Company, 1912.

DuVal, Kathleen. *Independence Lost: Lives on the Edge of the American Revolution*. New York: Random House, 2015.

Edelson, S. Max. *The New Map of Empire: How Britain Imagined America Before Independence.* Cambridge: Harvard University Press, 2017.

Gannon, Michael V. "Mitres and Flags: Colonial Religion in the British and Second Spanish Periods." In *Eighteenth-Century Florida: The Impact of the American Revolution*, edited by Samuel Proctor, 76–92. Gainesville: University Presses of Florida, 1978.

Gold, Pleasant Daniel. *History of Duval County Including Early History of East Florida.* St. Augustine: The Record Company, 1929.

Greene, Jack P. "The Role of the Lower Houses of Assembly in Eighteenth-Century Politics." *The Journal of Southern History* 27, no. 4 (November 1961): 451–474.

Henige, David P. *Colonial Governors from the Fifteenth Century to the Present.* Madison: The University of Wisconsin Press, 1970.

Herrmann, Rachel B. *No Useless Mouth: Waging War and Fighting Hunger in the American Revolution.* Ithaca: Cornell University Press, 2019.

The Historical Marker Database. The Rosario Defense Line Marker, St. Augustine, Florida 32084. 29° 53.799' N, 81° 18.885' in St. Johns County. https://www.hmdb.org/m.asp?m=47063

Hoffman, Paul E. *Florida's Frontiers.* Bloomington: Indiana University Press, 2002.

Lewis, James A. *The Final Campaign of the American Revolution: Rise and Fall of the Spanish Bahamas.* Columbia: University of South Carolina Press.

Lockey, Joseph B. "The Florida Banditti, 1783." *The Florida Historical Quarterly* 24, no. 2 (October 1945): 87–107.

Lynch, Wayne. "Button Gwinnett and Lachlan McIntosh Duel." *Journal of the American Revolution.* 24 September 2014. https://allthingsliberty.com/2014/09/button-gwinnett-and-the-mcintosh-duel/.

Lynch, Wayne. "Daniel McGirth, Banditti on the Southern Frontier." *Journal of the American Revolution.* 23 August 2016. https://allthingsliberty.com/2016/08/daniel-mcgirth-banditti-southern-frontier/.

Lynch, Wayne. "James Screven – Ambushed!" *Journal of the American Revolution.* 13 March 2014. https://allthingsliberty.com/2014/03/james-screven-ambushed/.

Manucy, Albert. "Changing Traditions in St. Augustine Architecture." In *Eighteenth-Century Florida: The Impact of the American Revolution,* edited by Samuel Proctor, 99–132. Gainesville: University Presses of Florida, 1978.

Marley, David F. *Wars of the Americas: A Chronology of Armed Conflict in the New World, 1492 to the Present.* Denver: ABC-CLIO, 1998.

Mays, David D. "Theatre Can't Get Here from There: A Brief Production History of Florida's First Play." In *Eighteenth-Century Florida: Life on the Frontier,* edited by Samuel Proctor, 91–100. Gainesville: The University Presses of Florida, 1976.

Mowat, Charles Loch. *East Florida as a British Province, 1763–1784.* 1943. Reprint. London: Forgotten Books, 2018.

Mowat, Charles L. "The Tribulations of Denys Rolle." *The Florida Historical Quarterly* 23, no. 1 (July 1944): 1–14.

Narrett, David. *Adventurism and Empire: The Struggle for Mastery in the Louisiana-Florida Borderlands, 1762–1803.* Chapel Hill: The University of North Carolina Press, 2015.

Nelson, Paul David. *General James Grant: Scottish Soldier and Royal Governor of East Florida.* Gainesville: University Press of Florida, 1993.

Nester, William R. *The Frontier War for American Independence.* Mechanicsburg: Stackpole Books, 2004.

O'Donnell III, James H. "The Florida Revolutionary Indian Frontier: Abode of the Blessed or Field of Battle?" In *Eighteenth-Century Florida: Life on the Frontier,* edited by Samuel Proctor, 60–74. Gainesville: The University Presses of Florida, 1976.

O'Shaughnessy, Andrew Jackson. *The Men Who Lost America: British Leadership, the American Revolution, and the Fate of the Empire.* New Haven: Yale University Press, 2013.

Olson, Gary D. "Thomas Brown, the East Florida Rangers, and the Defense of East Florida." In *Eighteenth-Century Florida and the Revolutionary South,* edited by Samuel Proctor, 15–28. Gainesville: The University Presses of Florida, 1978.

Panagopoulos, Epaminondas P. *New Smyrna: An Eighteenth Century Greek Odyssey.* Gainesville: University of Florida Press, 1966.

The Parliamentary History of England, from the Earliest Period to the Year 1803. Volume XV. London: R. Bagshaw, 1813.

Pennington, Edgar Legare. "East Florida in the American Revolution, 1775–1778." *The Florida Historical Quarterly* 9, no. 1 (July 1930): 24–46.

Piecuch, Jim. "Patrick Tonyn: Britain's Most Effective Revolutionary-Era Royal Governor." *Journal of the American Revolution*. 22 March 2018. https://allthingsliberty.com/2018/03/patrick-tonyn-britains-most-effective-revolutionary-era-royal-governor/.

Piecuch, Jim. *Three Peoples, One King: Loyalists, Indians, and Slaves in the Revolutionary South, 1775–1782*. Columbia: The University of South Carolina Press, 2008.

Raab, James W. *Spain, Britain and the American Revolution in Florida, 1763–1783*. Jefferson: McFarland & Company, 2008.

Rogers Jr., George C. "The East Florida Society of London." *The Florida Historical Quarterly* 54, no. 4 (April 1976): 479–496.

Schafer, Daniel L. "Chapter Eight: Of Engineers and Cartographers." *El Escribano: The St. Augustine Journal of History: St. Augustine's British Years 1763–1784* 38 (2001): 100–117.

Schafer, Daniel L. "Chapter Eleven: Men at Odds." *El Escribano: The St. Augustine Journal of History: St. Augustine's British Years 1763–1784* 38 (2001): 169–188.

Schafer, Daniel L. "Chapter Fifteen: 'realizing something out of the Wreck.'" *El Escribano: The St. Augustine Journal of History: St. Augustine's British Years 1763–1784* 38 (2001): 252–272.

Schafer, Daniel L. "Chapter Five: Governing the Town." *El Escribano: The St. Augustine Journal of History: St. Augustine's British Years 1763–1784* 38 (2001): 48–58.

Schafer, Daniel L. "Chapter Four: 'sharers of the wicked bottle.'" *El Escribano: The St. Augustine Journal of History: St. Augustine's British Years 1763–1784* 38 (2001): 41–47.

Schafer, Daniel L. "Chapter Fourteen: The Fate of East Florida." *El Escribano: The St. Augustine Journal of History: St. Augustine's British Years 1763–1784* 38 (2001): 230–251.

Schafer, Daniel L. "Chapter Nine: 'A sensible Clever man'-The Rise and Fall of Andrew Turnbull." *El Escribano: The St. Augustine Journal of History: St. Augustine's British Years 1763–1784* 38 (2001): 118–151.

Schafer, Daniel L. "Chapter One: 'not an herb, not a cabbage, all is overgrown with weeds.'" *El Escribano: The St. Augustine Journal of History: St. Augustine's British Years 1763–1784* 38 (2001): 4–15.

Schafer, Daniel L. "Chapter Seven: An Evolving Indian Policy." *El Escribano: The St. Augustine Journal of History: St. Augustine's British Years 1763–1784* 38 (2001): 76–99.

Schafer, Daniel L. "Chapter Six: The Royal Botanist and the St. Johns River." *El Escribano: The St. Augustine Journal of History: St. Augustine's British Years 1763–1784* 38 (2001): 59–75.

Schafer, Daniel L. "Chapter Ten: Acting Governor John Moultrie." *El Escribano: The St. Augustine Journal of History: St. Augustine's British Years 1763–1784* 38 (2001): 152–168.

Schafer, Daniel L. "Chapter Thirteen: A 'secure Asylum.'" *El Escribano: The St. Augustine Journal of History: St. Augustine's British Years 1763–1784* 38 (2001): 207–229.

Schafer, Daniel L. "Chapter Three: 'till this new world has in some means been created.'" *El Escribano: The St. Augustine Journal of History: St. Augustine's British Years 1763–1784* 38 (2001): 28–40.

Schafer, Daniel L. "Chapter Twelve: War on the Border." *El Escribano: The St. Augustine Journal of History: St. Augustine's British Years 1763–1784* 38 (2001): 189–206.

Schafer, Daniel L. "Chapter Two: 'Peopling & settling the new Established Colonies.'" *El Escribano: The St. Augustine Journal of History: St. Augustine's British Years 1763–1784* 38 (2001): 16–27.

Schafer, Daniel L. "Early Plantation Development in British East Florida." *El Escribano: The St. Augustine Journal of History* 19 (1982): 37–53.

Schafer, Daniel L. "Governor James Grant's Villa: A British East Florida Indigo Plantation." *El Escribano: The St. Augustine Journal of History* 37 (2000): 1–120.

Searcy, Martha Condray. *The Georgia-Florida Contest in the American Revolution, 1776–1778*. Tuscaloosa: The University of Alabama Press, 1985.

Sheridan, Richard B. "The British Sugar Planters and the Atlantic World, 1763–1775." In *Eighteenth-Century Florida and the Caribbean*, edited by Samuel Proctor, 1–14. Gainesville: The University Presses of Florida, 1976.

Siebert, Wilbur Henry. *Loyalists in East Florida, 1774–1785*. Volume I. 1929. Reprint. Greenville: Southern Historical Press.

Siebert, Wilbur Henry. "Slavery and White Servitude in East Florida, 1726–1776." *The Florida Historical Quarterly* 10, no. 1 (July 1931): 3–23.

Siebert, Wilbur Henry. *The Legacy of the American Revolution to the British West Indies and Bahamas: A Chapter out of the History of the American Loyalists*. Boston: Gregg Press, 1972.

Smith, Dr. Roger. *Hope of Freedom: Southern Blacks and the American Revolution.* St. Augustine: Colonial Research Associates, 2015.

Smith, Dr. Roger. *The 14th Colony: The American Revolution's Best Kept Secret.* St. Augustine: Colonial Research Associates, 2011.

Smith, W. Calvin. "Mermaids Riding Alligators: Divided Command on the Southern Frontier, 1776–1778." *The Florida Historical Quarterly* 54, no. 4 (April 1976): 443–464.

Sturgill, Claude C., ed. *The Humble Petition of Denys Rolle, Esq; setting forth the Hardships, Inconveniencies, and Grievances, which have attended him in his Attempts to make a Settlement in East Florida, humbly praying such Relief, as in their Lordships Wisdom shall seem meet, 1765.* Gainesville: The University Presses of Florida, 1977.

Tanner, Helen Hornbeck. "Pipesmoke and Muskets: Florida Indian Intrigues of the Revolutionary Era." In *Eighteenth-Century Florida and Its Borderlands*, edited by Samuel Proctor, 13–39. Gainesville: The University Presses of Florida, 1975.

Troxler, Carole Watterson. "Loyalist Refugees and the British Evacuation of East Florida, 1783–1785." *The Florida Historical Quarterly* 60, no. 1 (July 1981): 1–28.

Turner, Samuel P. "Maritime Insights from St. Augustine's British Period." *El Escribano: The St. Augustine Journal of History* 47 (2010): 1–21.

Walpole, Horace. *Memoirs of the Reign of King George III.* Volume I. London: Lawrence and Bullen, 1894.

Williams, Linda K. "East Florida as a Loyalist Haven." *The Florida Historical Quarterly* 54, no. 4 (April 1976): 465–478.

Wright, J. Leitch. "British East Florida: Loyalist Bastion." In *Eighteenth-Century Florida: The Impact of the American Revolution*, edited by Samuel Proctor, 1–13. Gainesville: University Presses of Florida, 1978.

Wright Jr., J. Leitch. "Blacks in British East Florida." *The Florida Historical Quarterly* 54, no. 4 (April 1976): 425–442.

Wright Jr., J. Leitch. *British St. Augustine.* St. Augustine: Historic St. Augustine Preservation Board, 1975.

Wright Jr., J. Leitch. *Florida in the American Revolution.* Gainesville: The University Press of Florida, 1975.

Index